STATE OF THE HEART

State of the Heart

South Carolina Writers on the Places They Love

VOLUME 3

EDITED BY AÏDA ROGERS

FOREWORD BY NIKKY FINNEY

AFTERWORD BY CASSANDRA KING

THE UNIVERSITY OF SOUTH CAROLINA PRESS

© 2018 University of South Carolina

Published by the University of South Carolina Press
Columbia, South Carolina 29208

www.sc.edu/uscpress

Manufactured in the United States of America

27 26 25 24 23 22 21 20 19 18
10 9 8 7 6 5 4 3 2 1

The Library of Congress Cataloging-in-Publication Data
can be found at http://catalog.loc.gov/.

ISBN 978-1-61117-902-6 (cloth)
ISBN 978-1-61117-903-3 (paperback)
ISBN 978-1-61117-904-0 (ebook)

"The Rent We Pay for Living" excerpted in parts from *Lanterns: A Memoir of Mentors*
© 1999 by Marian Wright Edelman. Beacon Press Boston. Published under the auspices
of the Unitarian Universalist Association of Congregations. www.beacon.org.

My wound is geography. It is also my anchorage, my port of call.

Pat Conroy, *The Prince of Tides*

Contents

ILLUSTRATIONS

One never knows when or where a true place will be found—a true place being somewhere our heart recognizes as just right then leaps into song, or suddenly and without warning rockets quietly out of our chest. When I was a girl, the edges of my grandparents' pond were a true place. The sensualist in me was born in the arms of its muddy water, my toes always half in, half out. Without the sensualist of then, there would be no poet of now. This is not a blues song, but it was the muddy red water of South Carolina that taught me how to put one foot in front of the other and push off in search of the rest of my horizon. Back then on the shores of this watery land, I began to hear something, something I had no idea I would need to hear for the rest of my life, if I had hope of spending it in a long dance with words.

In Conway, South Carolina, the salty waves of the Atlantic covered me like a daily slippery caul, from that first kicking breath of birth to a few years later when I began to move upright in the world. Next door to this first body of water, on the seashell strand where my ancestors first stepped off slave ships or perhaps were pushed off to their knees, was where I learned to walk. This coastal water was the historic baptizing water of the South Carolina lowcountry. This coastal water took me to the next sacred water high in the upstate, where I walked ancient creeks that poked and hid deep down in the woods of my grandparents' farm in Newberry, South Carolina. In my second decade of life, a muddy pond was cut out of the ground by my grandfather's hands and back, with the help of farm agents from the county extension office, which was looking for farmers, like my grandfather, who wanted to embark on a new rural enterprise alongside the staple crops of corn and soybean. My grandmother slipped a fishing pole in my hand.

I didn't like to fish. I didn't like to see any living thing upside down, struggling with a hook in its mouth. But I had to say I was going fishing in order to stare at everything else going on at the pond. To get there I had to walk due west, some five hundred yards from out of the small stone house my grandfather had built with his back and hands. Once at the barbed-wire fence, I would take both hands to hold open the top and bottom wires until they jawed wide enough for my long legs and then contort first my head, then the middle of my body, my nine-year-old piney legs, and my bamboo pole all clear and through to the pond side. I would release the wire carefully behind me and climb the small ridge of powdery, ochre-red dirt, walking straight down to the edges of the lapping pond, where finally the adults back at the house could not see me anymore. There I would squat and take my place with other living things.

In the arms of this muddy red water, circa late 1960s, I stood and began my lifelong education into the lost art of thinking way too much about the world of what I believed were mostly overlooked things and beings. With my heels and toes anchored into the mud, the fake red worm now on the hook and hidden somewhere in the dark throat of the middle of the pond, I would spend hours marveling at the shore around my toes, uninterested in the worm or the catgut string or my hands clasped around the lip of the bamboo pole. I preferred to stare at the edge of the muddy water, where a complex system of insect life was all around me. There were ice-skating insects and trembling tadpoles and frogs moving through the warm water's edge, all in liquid flight. This mud hole, this pond of bug sounds and swirls, was where I learned to feel the zoom of my heart and to weigh it against the broken scales of the noisy, beckoning otherworld outside its banks. This sensory-rich, true place led me to other sensory-rich, true places.

At nine I didn't know anything for sure, but I felt everything for sure. I knew nothing about the physiology of the heart, but I knew I could hear mine best when my feet were in red muddy water. I could feel mine best when anchored in time with the jazz of life there on the pond. In the years that followed, I learned that the heart beats one hundred thousand times a day. I read somewhere that the right side of the heart pumps blood to the lungs in order to pick up oxygen and that the left side of the heart receives the oxygen-rich blood only to pump it out democratically to the rest of the body. I learned that if I placed my open palm up under my seersucker blouse, I could feel the pounding in my chest heading through the outlets of my fingers and deeper into my body. Whatever my heart knows today has everything to do with opening that barbed wire with my bare hands, sitting at that muddy pond with my toes bare, and studying those hard-working insects with my staring eyes. That time at the pond, away from the chores of everyday arm-and-leg work back at the house, situated me in the deep true place of my interior self.

There is physical geography and there is human geography, and they are not unrelated. By its very definition, geography means "to describe the earth." *State of the Heart* is a report from the frontlines of South Carolina's physical and human earth. It is a book of portraits and landscapes that are meant to tell the story of what matters to the people who are telling them. Long before the modern phenomenon of Google Earth began to take pictures of planet earth, we humans worked without satellite help, with only pen and paper, to document where in the world we were and why it mattered to the spider web of life. The cameras necessary for that old way of telling had already been deeply set inside us at birth, and we used them alongside our long memories. *State of the Heart* is a report from where many of us have stopped to weigh our hearts once again. Here in these pages you will discover just how much a heart can weigh, just how tall a heart can rise and fly, once it remembers its true place.

Nikky Finney

ACKNOWLEDGMENTS

Stingy people don't contribute to anthologies. Nor do stingy publishers publish them. So big thanks and "great love"—as Pat Conroy would say—to Nikky Finney, Cassandra King, and all the writers whose stories appear here, and to Jonathan Haupt and the University of South Carolina Press for bringing them to you.

We live in a small and complicated state, but there's nothing small or complicated about artists and photographers who donate their work and time so graciously for a book that won't bring them a cent. Likewise, there's no group of people more helpful, more necessary, than the librarians, historians, and archivists who drop what they're doing to help a sleuthing editor find what she needs. Those behind-the-scenes pros and others need to be named and praised: Bill Allen with Allen Brothers Milling Company; Beth Bilderback at USC's South Caroliniana Library; Tom Clark with the South Carolina Film Commission; Mary Doyle with the Sea Pines Resort; Judge John Flythe in Augusta; Selden "Bud" Hill with the Village Museum in McClellanville; Lucy Quinn with the Greenville County Historical Society; Robin Salmon with Brookgreen Gardens; Lynn Sky with Blue Sky Gallery; Michele Smith, special assistant to the president at the Children's Defense Fund; Angela Stump with the John Carroll Doyle Art Gallery; and Natalie Titcomb with the Drayton Hall Preservation Trust. Harlan Greene, head of special collections at the College of Charleston's Addlestone Library, who so generously contributed to volume 2, helped locate images of the puzzlingly hard-to-find Elizabeth O'Neill Verner. Special thanks to photographer Allen Anderson for accepting the difficult, time-consuming task of taking a photo of a painting and to Elizabeth Ward with the Ward Law Firm in Columbia for letting him do so. New Ellenton town councilman Ron Reynolds tried tirelessly to help me find reproducible images of his community. He did not succeed, but I got a new friend and yet more proof of how kind strangers can be. (And don't get me started on the importance of taking photos of people and places and making sure they're stored for eternity—or at least for the next tribe of detectives curious about these lands and waters.)

I'm beyond lucky to have wonderful friends and family who either help me or leave me alone as this book progresses. Tracy Fredrychowski patiently deals with my panic when it comes to high-tech graphics and photography. Friends Nancy Allison, Cam Currie, Kathy Henry Dowell, Sharon Kelly, Gene Lammers, and Joy Simpson, and my sister Myda Tompkins and mother Maro Rogers help me with proofing. My most able eyeballer is my father, Hugh Rogers. My most able enabler is my husband, Wally Peters. Wally is a professor of mechanical engineering. Thanks to him, everything heats, cools, runs, and flushes while I endeavor on my projects. There would be no book without him.

When I put together the first collection, I didn't know there might be more. So I didn't realize I'd need to keep looking for pertinent images and corresponding quotes and literary passages for the "section introduction pages." I've had enormous fun combing through South Carolina books, websites, and photo collections—and museums, galleries, and eBay postcards—but finding just the right match of words and art is more time-consuming than some might think. For this volume I turned to several writers who contributed to the first one. From books they'd already written came help from Billy Baldwin, Tom Poland, and that "proud South Carolinian" gone too soon, Ken Burger. Nick Lindsay rescued me with his oral history of Edisto Island. Tom Johnson, who contributed to volume 2, led me to James McBride Dabbs, that "man of letters and lettuce" whose writings I've come to love. I also found my way to "Heaven" by the late Starkey Flythe Jr. What a gift he left for us, in just four stanzas.

I'm incredibly grateful to Dot Jackson, Dinah Johnson, and Deno Trakas, all of whom composed original work when I asked. But that should surprise no one. They, and everyone connected to this effort, are generosity personified. As the great Dorothy Gale once said, "You're the best friends anybody could ever have."

INTRODUCTION *Custom-Made*

On Thursday, November 8, 1956, arguably the most beautiful and exotic woman ever to come to Lexington, South Carolina, stood on Church Street trying to leave. Not for good. She just needed the afternoon. The deadline of her life was that Sunday, and if she was going to meet it, she needed to make that four o'clock Greyhound to Columbia.

It's doubtful she paid any attention to the art moderne station once she stepped off the bus at 1200 Blanding Street, or to the Depression modern Tapp's department store on the next block, where she was headed. She was focused on the bridal department, where she plunked down $150 for a wedding dress—taffeta with a ballerina skirt—and a pink nightgown with matching housecoat. Then back to the station on Blanding and home to Lexington, where she'd teach high school civics, history, and English the next day before returning to Columbia in the afternoon. A Tapp's seamstress would have made alterations to the dress, and then there was the matter of Daddy's ring. Forty dollars for that, and she was done. She'd be at the altar of Lexington Methodist Church on time and under budget, her ponytail intact, the orchid on her prayer book secure. Waiting for her there was my father in his army uniform, his brother in his only suit, and Dr. R. Wright Spears, president of Columbia College, who'd happily agreed to officiate at the wedding of his first foreign student. There hadn't been much planning—Daddy was shipping out soon for Korea—but the church was packed. That happened in a small town when a teacher married a local who was the cousin of half the people there.

Here's the thing: if my mother had had the time and a sewing machine, she would have made the dress herself. She would have stepped off that bus in Columbia and had it been a year later, marched to Chez Fabrique on Main Street, searched through patterns and bolts of material, and come up with her own design. She'd already made a snappy little sundress for herself—white linen with a red-and-white polka-dotted sash—using a borrowed pattern from her CC roommate and a campus sewing machine. It cost her $1.49. For glamour and thrift, you couldn't beat Maro Kouyoumjian Rogers, formerly of Baghdad, forever after of Lexington.

We grew up with her mindset, her "I can make that for ten dollars" when we'd see dresses for much more. Our homemade outfits, to me, were just that—homemade, proof that we were poor. I didn't reconcile her hours at the shiny black Modernage precision sewing machine—seventy-six dollars when Daddy bought it in Charleston in 1958—with the money saved and those drive-through trips to the bank, Mom's hand dropping an envelope in the drawer "for your college." It took me years to realize that her work on our dresses—and our bedspreads, our curtains, our wool plaid coats with the matching velvet bonnets—had everything in common with my work writing stories. Pins in her mouth, cuss words in mine, we gather our material and piece things together, inching toward a deadline on something that might work or might not. We choose our patterns then abandon them halfway, detour in unplanned directions and tack on odd notions. Whole sleeves and paragraphs are built and destroyed, big messes left gaping to be salvaged another day. It's a maddening business, sewing and writing. Mama would scream. I still do.

I don't know how much wreckage occurred with these stories before they came to me, all polished and professional. I do know good writers make hard work look easy. And mothers take their children places and teach them things they never forget. Could there have been a more exciting place than the thronging sidewalks of Main Street Columbia in the 1960s, crossing diagonally from one department store to the next, holding your sister's hand or your mother's? Was there ever a happier hubbub than in Tapp's Downtown, with its clatter of cosmetics on the first floor and the din of diners in its basement restaurant? Even the wallpaper in Tapp's Fountain Room restaurant was big-city—the figures of stylish women like those on the patterns Mom bought to sew. And Chez Fabrique—its own Aladdin's cave of color and texture, ruffles and ribbon, where little girls could look at and touch the floor-to-ceiling bolts of cloth, stare at the wall of sequins and lace, pronounce such words of deliciousness: Brocade. Organza. *Chiffon.*

Anne Knight Watson in McClellanville runs the Village Stitchers, a group who knit prayer blankets for those who are sick. I barely knew Anne

Knight when I asked her for one. Mama had gotten sick, dangerously so, and the family sprawled after her, to doctors, hospitals, more doctors, more hospitals. Anne Knight brought me a blanket, watermelon-red trimmed in moss green. It followed my mother everywhere, from hospital to nursing home to rehab center, into ambulances and deep into her "crazy days," my sister calls them, the long months when she couldn't walk, couldn't talk, hardly ate. In that otherworld of surgeries and infections, IVs and beeping machines, she lost her English and forty pounds, her knees and nose gaining prominence while the rest of her receded. She began looking like the Armenian refugees from whom she descended half a world away.

For me the numbness was pierced by two things. The first was joyous relief to learn Kathy Sons—Hinkle now—was the head nurse of the wing at the nursing home where Mom was being cared for. Kathy Sons, my older sister's classmate, with whom we'd endured years of Mrs. Christine B. Ingram's agonizing spring piano recitals in the dark and creaky auditorium of Lexington Elementary School. She *knew us.* The second was rage when Surgeon Number One, perhaps covering for Surgeon Number Two, told me, pointedly, that people twenty years old didn't survive the surgery my mother, at eighty-three, would be facing the next day.

But she did. And when I brought her home for good, she sat down at the kitchen table and asked me to bring her a needle and thread. She'd remembered the filter in the dryer had torn, and it was bugging her. She needed to fix it. Seven months after that, she and my father visited us in McClellanville. I pointed out Anne Knight's house when we drove through the village, and then Anne Knight herself at T. W. Graham's, the restaurant there. Gripping her cane, my mother moved forward to introduce herself. "You don't know me," she began, and thanked her for the blanket. I stood back and watched them, the knitter and the sewer, laughing and talking and shaking hands the way women do. But I think Anne Knight did know Mama. She knew her, the way knitters weave their blankets, writers sew their stories, and families tend each other, in sickness and in health, no matter how it ends.

Egrets at Dawn. Watercolor by Mary Whyte. Photograph courtesy of the artist.

Morning

Where ocean meets sky
infinity ends, morning
comes: Carolina.

Deno Trakas

A Scrap of Heaven

Miss Larkin passed away on a hazy fall morning. Goldenrod bent low beneath skittering dragonflies, and the South Carolina air, sodden and thick, pressed down on the Spartina grass that clung to the creek's edge just outside her house. It was the same tidal creek that had eased by for nine decades, past the tire swing, the vague footprint of a garden, and the two oak trees that were frequently strung with rows of damp work shirts and colorful quilts lifting skyward in the breeze. The creek had been Miss Larkin's touchstone, held between the seasons like an unfinished hymn, alongside the place where babies were born and anger buried. That morning the outgoing tide slowed by her house, pausing to retrace the small swirls as if confused, inquiring, listening for the thin breath exhaled. It wasn't until three hours later, when the sun had filled the sky and the tide had emptied the creeks to the welcoming arms of the sea, that I received the phone call.

For most of my adult life I have lived in my own little house by the marsh. My husband and I originally moved from the Northeast, heading south to find warmth and sustenance, becoming two unlikely migratory birds that stayed behind. Since then we have marked the years by the movement of the estuaries and the creatures that call it home, noting the tide's twice-daily push inland and its subsequent retreat to the horizon. We have watched otters gliding through the water, tossing oyster shells off their glistening stomachs in summer, and mergansers paddling through the frigid agate tide in winter. On rainy days the creeks are sullen, but on a clear night under a full moon the water turns to platinum, with minuscule fish churning the surface into a spray of diamonds. Year round the king-fishers chatter and duel for their provision among the leaping mullet, and

3

thumbnail-sized snails travel up and down the slender marsh grass skimming the rise and fall of the tide. A few summers ago, a visiting friend's young son gathered a few of the snails for his aquarium in Ohio, where the tiny creatures continued their lowcountry vigil up and down the reeds to the precise rhythm of the tides.

At night the marsh weaves its way in and out of our dreams. The creek passes by less than a hundred feet from our bedroom window, where we can hear the splash of deer and the occasional calling of an owl from somewhere high in the pine trees above. Raccoons prowl for unsecured garbage cans, and opossums white as marble rustle through the grasses and under the house carrying their clinging babies. One night we heard the mating of two bobcats in the pampas grass just off our deck. The yowling screams were both terrifying and primordial, sending our golden retriever scrambling to his feet, the silhouette of his back and neck jagged and upright in the moonlight. It was a sound made of life and death, and as piercing as lightning over the ocean. The dog was never the same again.

For all these years, I have walked along the marsh almost every morning and have occasionally witnessed beauty so startling I had to race back to my studio to fetch my palette and brushes. I have painted the sky turning from violet to turquoise, crisscrossed with the silver gashes of jet trails, as well as thunderheads as rounded and pink as a cluster of wild roses. At low tide I have set up my easel in the pluff mud, painting banks of bleached oysters among the rivulets or the reflection of the sky in the shallow pools, as pretty and as blue as a robin's egg. In winter, when morning walks require a long, swishing coat, the sketchbook remains in my pocket against my hand. Even if I don't stop to draw, ideas are saved for the solitude and comfort of my studio, where I can freely conjure muses and hot tea for the day's work ahead.

The morning Miss Larkin passed away, I was walking to Jenkins Point, the narrow arm of Seabrook Island that reaches across the wide expanse of tidelands toward the North Edisto River. The sun, rosy and soft as the inside of a doe's mouth, had nudged its way over the top of the trees, turning the marsh the color of cotton candy. I stopped near a pond to watch the awakening egrets as they gurgled and fluttered their wings, shaking off the dew. One by one the egrets lifted off from their low perches, beating upward, then headed west in a floating string toward the river and the fertile marsh flats. As they took off, a watery reflection answered and slipped by beneath them, an ascending strand of white pearls in search of shimmering fish.

I felt the phone buzz in my pocket, and held it to my ear. Eartha Lee's voice came, halting, silent, then starting again. It is a voice I recognized from the sisterhood I have painted for more than twenty years. Most of the women are decades older than I and can name ancestors that lived on these barrier islands long before they became the dominion of waterfront mansions. Theirs are the voices of Gullah spirituals born from hope and backbreaking toil on the plantations generations ago. They have earned their crowns of silver hair, with stockings puddling around ankles that have walked through a lifetime of adversity. Each week for decades, they've met at a Johns Island church, first for Bible study, then hunched over expanding quilts that smell of Spanish moss and rain. Often the squares of fabric are the remnants of old clothing, a commodity of purpose and sanctification.

It is eighty-year-old Eartha Lee's position to lead the group's weekly meetings, to remember the birthdays and the hospital visits, and to notify the members of a break in the chain. Her voice caught and stopped, searching to find the right words.

"I know," I said softly, holding the phone to my ear and watching the birds streaming overhead. "I know."

The sky had turned the color of a faded blue dress drying in the breeze when the last egret rose from the pond. The pumping wings turned iridescent in the sun, gaining force, as the bird ascended and veered off from the others, drifting high into the clouds over the river. The egret circled once, hesitated, and then disappeared into the widening expanse. ☽

Junior League officers, Columbia, 1949–51. Photograph by John Hensel, courtesy of the South Caroliniana Library, University of South Carolina, Columbia.

Town People

"In small towns, you're never out of your mother's sight. Or somebody else's mother's."

Ken Burger (1949–2015), from "Raised by a Hundred Mothers," collected in *Baptized in Sweet Tea*

)

The Rent We Pay for Living

The black-white duality of my South Carolina childhood, upbringing, and passage to adulthood shaped my trajectory in life. I remember as a four-year-old child being snatched away from a whites-only drinking fountain in Belk's department store on Main Street in Bennettsville and discovering there was such a thing as "white" and "black" water. I chafed a few years later at being denied entrance to the public library. (I am *so* proud that the beautiful new Marlboro County Public Library has been named for me, with big letters at the entrance saying, "Welcome to Everyone.") I remember other things: not understanding why I couldn't sit down at drugstore lunch counters when I could purchase anything else in the store, resenting the hand-me-down books in our separate-but-unequal black public school, and standing in a big crowd of white adults hearing South Carolina governor James Byrnes say on the Marlboro County Courthouse lawn that black children would *never* go to school with white children.

Happily the external constraints in my segregated childhood were tempered by steady messages of high parental expectation and positive black community support.

Life was not easy in the 1940s and 1950s in rural South Carolina for many black children, as the outside world told us we weren't important. But our parents said it wasn't so, our teachers said it wasn't so, and my daddy the preacher said it wasn't so. So I knew it wasn't so.

We always had books in my home so that the whole world was open to the Wright children. My daddy sat for hours every day reading in his book-lined church study and took us to see and hear great black role models sing or speak within 150 miles of our home so that we would know there was a bigger world of possibility to aspire to and heroes to emulate. So I

Arthur Jerome Wright and Maggie Leola Bowen Wright. Photos courtesy of
Marian Wright Edelman

have always believed I could help change the world, because I have been
lucky to have been exposed to adults around me who did—in small and
large ways. How lucky I feel to have been born at a time and place of great
transforming events and transformative leaders who became my teachers
and leaders.

So while life was often hard and resources scarce, we Wright children
always knew who we were and that the measure of our worth was inside
our heads and hearts and not outside in possessions or worldly values. I
was taught that the world had a lot of problems; that black people had
an extra lot of problems but were able and obligated to struggle and
change them; that being poor was no excuse for not achieving; and that
extra intellectual and material gifts brought with them the privilege and
responsibility of sharing with others less fortunate. And we learned that
education was the key to success. My daddy, as he lay dying in an ambulance, reminded me one last time to let nothing get between me and my
education. And his and my mother's lives taught daily that service is the
rent we pay for living—it is the very purpose of life and not something
you do in your spare time—and that those of us with an education have a
responsibility to lift others. I am so grateful for these priceless childhood
lessons and legacies.

Shiloh Baptist Church. Photograph courtesy of Shiloh Baptist Church.

My belief that I and all of us can do more than complain, wring hands, or give in to despair at the wrongs rife in the world stems from my parents' examples. Daddy, a teacher-preacher who never raised his voice in the pulpit, tried to educate our congregation's minds as well as touch their hearts. He taught that faith required action and that action could be sustained only by faith in the face of daily discouragement and injustice in our segregated southern society. When you see a need, he said, don't ask why someone doesn't do something; ask what you can do and do it.

Because the public playgrounds and swimming pools and most public services like the library in Bennettsville were closed to black children, Mama and Daddy made our church, Shiloh Baptist, a hub for children. Boy and Girl Scout troops, a skating rink, a small canteen behind the church to make up for the segregated lunch counters, ball games and other physical activities provided outlets for pent-up child energy. Choirs, children's days, baby contests, Miss Universe pageants, and vacation Bible school made church a welcoming haven and leadership incubator rather than a boring chore. And the great preachers and teachers invited to speak at Shiloh helped challenge our minds and widen our horizons and remind us that there were rainbows in the clouds.

My parents made sure that we were exposed to as many great role models as possible. Dr. Benjamin E. Mays from Ninety Six, South Carolina, came and stayed at our parsonage when he was president of Morehouse College and spoke at Shiloh. Dr. Mays shaped many thousands of young black leaders during his years at Morehouse, including Dr. Martin Luther King Jr., my brother Harry, and me. My parents took me as a young girl to have dinner at Benedict College with Dr. Mary McLeod Bethune, a Mayesville, South Carolina, native, president of Bethune Cookman College in Florida and founder of the National Council of Negro Women. I was awed by her as she commanded a roomful of men, and it was from her that night that I first heard "the blacker the berry, the sweeter the juice" as she affirmed her self-acceptance and regaled us with stories of how she challenged racism at every opportunity, including trying on hats in white stores—usually forbidden.

My parents did not have to raise me and my sister and brothers alone, because children were viewed as community property. Every place I went, there were eyes watching and mouths reporting on me. When I strayed into places or company of which my parents didn't approve, those eyes and mouths went to work. Some of these wise community elders indelibly influenced my childhood. Miz Tee Kelly was one of them. She lived in a four-room unpainted house with a big front porch and a small back porch, every inch of it sparkling clean. Every Sunday night my family enjoyed Miz Tee's scrumptious dinners of fried or smothered chicken, macaroni and cheese, rice or mashed potatoes with gravy to die for, greens—collard, mustard, turnip, or cabbage—and the thickest but lightest buttermilk biscuits, the recipe for which she took to heaven with her, that would melt in my mouth. Topped off by the best sweet potato pone I've ever tasted and fresh churned ice cream, Miz Tee's dinners were a treasured Wright family ritual each Sabbath evening. Miz Tee's love followed me to Spelman College in Atlanta, and my friends on my dormitory floor waited for her shoeboxes full of fried chicken and biscuits and sweet potato pone with a greasy dollar bill or two included.

The grande dames of Bennettsville. Mrs. Theresa Kelly, or "Miz Tee," is in the center of the back row, wearing a black dress with white corsage. Photograph courtesy of the author.

As the last, and for six years the only, child at home, I usually accompanied my daddy on pastoral visits and my mother to her circles, Mothers' Club, and missionary society meetings, where I overheard the womenfolk's talk and gossip as we shared meals and engaged in various church and community chores. When my mother died thirty years after my daddy, an old white man asked me what I did. I realized in a flash that I do what my parents did—serve those left behind and treated unjustly—only on a bigger scale.

I miss the sense of community we shared back then. Because there were no washing machines or dryers, black women in Bennettsville washed their families' and white people's clothes in big washtubs, with scrub boards, soaked them in Rinso, washed out heavy stains with lye, hung them on clotheslines to dry, and pressed them with irons heated on wood- and coal-burning stoves. When the women came to our yard, I helped out by hanging up the well-rinsed wet clothes on lines, taking them down after they dried, and folding them. And every year black women of our community would gather at our parsonage to can fresh vegetables and fruit from gardens and farms, which got us through winter scarcity, and the men would gather on a church member's farm to kill hogs and prepare meats they stored in their smokehouses. Hog chitterlings took turns hanging on our parsonage clothesline.

I knew deep and persistent anger even as a very young child, and many of my struggles for children today stem from childhood incidents. Little Johnny Harrington, who lived three houses down from our church parsonage, died after he stepped on a nail and did not get a tetanus shot. Making sure every child gets immunizations and health care is a relentless lifelong passion of mine. Racial disparities in health care treatment became clear in an accident in front of our church on Cheraw Highway in the middle of the night, where a black migrant family and a white truck driver collided. The ambulance came, saw that the white truck driver was unhurt, and drove away although the black family members were seriously injured. I will never forget it. My parents took in foster children and started an old folks' home when an elderly minister lost his memory, roamed the streets, and had no place to go. My passion for justice seeded in my early years has grown stronger over time and will never cease.

In 2014 I was deeply honored to be inducted into the South Carolina Hall of Fame along with one of my great heroines, Mrs. Septima Clark. Mrs. Rosa Parks called Mrs. Clark the "mother of the civil rights movement." Mrs. Parks said she sat down just once, but Septima Clark repeatedly challenged racially discriminatory laws and practices, fought courageously for equal educational opportunity for children and equal pay for black teachers, and taught illiterate black citizens, beginning on Johns Island, South Carolina, how to read and to exercise their rights as voters. As a young civil rights lawyer, I was exposed to Matthew Perry and Ernest Finney Jr., cooperating attorneys with the NAACP Legal Defense Fund where I worked, also members of the South Carolina Hall of Fame, along with the great Dr. Mays and Dr. Bethune and my friend, former governor and US secretary of education Richard Riley. It was an extraordinary and unexpected honor—and a moving reminder of just how far South Carolina and the nation have come. But we are not where we must be as a state and nation yet, and the call for courageous service and leadership remains as urgent today if every child in South Carolina and in America is to be healthy, educated, safe, and able to see and seize the future.

The call today is to end morally obscene child poverty levels (14.7 million poor children), illiteracy, and violence in the biggest economy and most powerful military power on earth, which lets its children be the poorest group among us. Our failure to invest in and educate *all* our children will be our undoing unless we all pick up the baton Dr. Mays, Dr. Bethune, and Mrs. Clark passed on to us. ↄ

☾

A Tale of Two Towns

In 1962 my family moved to New Ellenton, a little one-stoplight town between Aiken and the Savannah River Plant, where my dad worked helping to manufacture plutonium for atomic bombs. The plant was run by the federal government and DuPont. I'm not quite sure how that marriage managed to work, but the plant filled my town with transplants from all over who had come to work at the bomb plant, or *bum plant*. Either pronunciation was perfectly acceptable.

As serious as what folks were doing out there was, my dad always had a sense of humor about himself. When I was in the third grade, I was supposed to ask him exactly what he did for a living and report back to the class during show and tell. This was tricky, since most everything at the Savannah River site was considered classified, but my dad gave me the answer. And not knowing any better, I stood up in front of the blackboard the next day and announced with pride, "My daddy taps the bombs with a hammer to see if they work." The whole class broke up laughing. After my mortification subsided, I forgave him and his sense of humor that helped him work forty hours a week with heavy water and elements from the periodic table that could blind you before they melted your face off.

I never remember being afraid of what might lie beyond the DuPont guard shack. Sure, I learned the word *classified* before the average kindergartener, but there was a kind of nonchalance about my dad and everyone I knew who worked there. After all, it was just plutonium. It wasn't like they were really tapping bombs with hammers.

While my life was never ruled by fear, it was ruled by the plant traffic. Highway 19 ran through town, four lanes cutting New Ellenton into two equal portions. There wasn't a single soul whose comings and goings weren't dictated by the DuPont traffic, a steady stream of bumper-to-bumper cars whizzing through town like clockwork over three shift changes.

When I was little, this constant was somewhat comforting, but as I got older, it was annoying. The plant traffic dictated whether my mom would let me cross the highway to play on the other side of town. The Piggly Wiggly, the bank, and the Eubanks' Esso station were on the sometimes-forbidden side, which really shouldn't have been so enticing since Rose's Five and Dime, the only store in town with cheap toys like old maid cards, jump ropes, and jacks, was on the safe side, but it was.

Thirteen miles north, Highway 19 also dissected Aiken, though not as evenly. Going to town with Mama was one of my first memories after moving to New Ellenton. The windows were rolled down, and I stood on the bench seat leaning into her while she drove with her left hand and held on to me with her right.

Even with Mama's lead foot, it seemed like it took forever to get to Aiken. Finally we were there, almost crawling down Whiskey Road, past humongous, stately magnolias. Their scent was sweet and heady and almost too much, and I remember thinking if Mama let go of me, I could hang out the window and touch their white velvet blossoms. Pick one of those large glossy green leaves that looked like someone had taken a dust rag and Pledge to every single tree.

And then the biggest homes ever came into view, with tiled roofs and fancy stone exteriors—a stark contrast to the cookie-cutter red-brick houses back home or the ones along the part of Whiskey Road that pared down from four lanes to two. Just the sight of those mansions made my imagination take off.

What would happen if Mama pulled our old white Ford Fairlane down one of those forbidden driveways that were so thick with tiny white pebbles the car would have surely bogged down? How many people lived in those houses? Where did they come from? Did they work at the bomb plant like everyone else I knew? Why did some of them want to keep the world out with ivy-covered stucco walls and fancy wrought-iron gates, while others showed off their long, unobstructed driveways? Did they have children? If they did, why weren't their bikes thrown down in their driveways or their toys strewn about their yards?

Not far from those mansions, and only on Sundays, there was always a sign out with a single word. *POLO.* There were no directions. I didn't know what polo was, but I knew that one word said, "If you have to ask,

South Boundary Avenue. Watercolor by Betsy Wilson-Mahoney. Courtesy of the artist.

you don't belong," which makes me a little sad today because I came out of my mother a horse girl. What a wonder that would have been watching high-dollar ponies gallop about, playing a game whose object wasn't much different than the croquet my sisters and I played with the set Mama got with Green Stamps at the Piggly Wiggly.

"Going to town" meant shopping on Laurens Street in Aiken with its pretty fountain and retail stores. In that area of town, there were scores of storybook cottages that looked so inviting and so different from the rough red dirt roads in the middle of the city that led to more mansions and more stables. As many times as I've seen a rider on horseback, waiting for the light to change to cross Whiskey Road and get to Hitchcock Woods, it is still as much of a wonder as driving through the oak-covered tunnel on South Boundary Avenue or past the serpentine wall on Whiskey Road.

I loved growing up in New Ellenton; it fueled my childhood with endless days on a bike, on horseback, on a red clay tennis court with a saggy net and no boundaries. It was where I began to write stories with a fat no. 2 pencil, and I've never stopped.

But early on, it was Aiken that fueled my imagination and took me to the place where story lives and breathes. One look at that serpentine wall, and she still takes me there today. ☽

Orville Vernon Burton

☽

Mystery and Contradiction

My Story of Ninety Six

Historians of the American South know the importance of place. As Eudora Welty suggests in *The Eye of the Story,* "One place comprehended can make us understand other places better. Sense of place gives equilibrium; extended, it is sense of direction." I have always appreciated the wonderful places I have lived (except perhaps basic training at Fort Bragg, North Carolina); every place offers something special and something to appreciate (and in hindsight, so did Fort Bragg). But ask a historian of the American South a question, and you will be told a story. Storytelling is partly what defines the South, and my story, and thus my heart, centers on Ninety Six, South Carolina. Some would say Ninety Six is my omphalos; it is certainly my story. After all, there is no place like home.

My family on both sides was from rural Georgia, although centuries before their families had migrated through South Carolina. During the Depression my mother left the farm in rural Madison County and accepted a job with neighbors and family friends who had a general store, including clothing merchandise, in Abbeville, South Carolina. My father lost his leg in the Marines, before World War II and penicillin. A bad amputation left him with an exposed nerve and in excruciating pain. In 1940 my mother and father married in Abbeville, where my mother was now managing the store. My father, determined to work, posted bond to become an insurance salesperson. Unfortunately he had to go into the veterans hospital, and to keep from losing the bond, my mother took the job and became one of the first women to run an insurance debit—going to the homes of the customers to collect weekly or monthly premiums. That is how my story of my Ninety Six begins.

I was not born in South Carolina, although my mother and father lived in Ninety Six. My father hated the Georgia demagogue Gene Talmadge so much he took my pregnant mother from their home in Ninety Six and drove some eighty miles across the Savannah River so I could be born near the family homeplace in rural Georgia and thus be in a better position to challenge Talmadge's son Herman for governor. (I never got this opportunity, as Gene Talmadge died when I was an infant in Ninety Six and Herman just sort of assumed the chief executive position.) I spent the first eighteen years of my life in Ninety Six, with frequent drives across the Georgia–South Carolina border to visit grandmothers. That was my life until I left for Furman University in 1965, then Princeton in 1969, then Urbana, Illinois, in 1974. Except for two brief stints in the army, my life since Ninety Six has been at universities, another irony, since neither my mother nor father had the opportunity to finish high school.

I was teaching at the University of Illinois when I met my wife. I told Georgeanne I was in Illinois temporarily, that I would soon be going home to the South. It was just as North Carolina native Charles Kuralt warned in his humorous poem "Barbecue Blues": "Young folks, think on that man's folly, / Before you board that bus in Raleigh." I had experienced, though I left Ninety Six on the train for Princeton, what Kuralt had expressed—the estrangement of many an expatriate who went north and discovered southernness. But more than craving a return to the South in general, I wanted to go home to Ninety Six. Another poem elicits my feelings, this one a song by Alabama. In "Down Home," the band sings about a place "where they know you by name and treat you like family /. . . down home."

It took thirty-four years, but I am now back home in Ninety Six. Of course Thomas Wolfe was right: "you can't go home again." Wolfe's protagonist returns home to discover no one can go back to a life "which once seemed everlasting" but of course is "changing all the time." Life means change, and history is the study of change over time. "We leave home, and are battered about by life, we are changed," *Time* magazine recently commented. "Home becomes a symbol of our innocence, a place where we dreamed limitlessly and were loved unconditionally. But that home, too, has changed because of our absence." True, perhaps, in so many ways, but I am living proof that you can never truly leave. You may do so physically or even intellectually, but never in spirit. Thus I have made a full circle and come home, or at least to a place, a state of the heart, I call home. Ninety Six will always hold my heart because of the fullness of its history, its sense of community, and the beauty of its landscape.

As a historian by trade, I find that the name "Ninety Six" calls out for historical explanation. Ninety Six is one of the oldest towns in the state. People who ask about the origin of its name will hear a romantic legend, which has some basis in fact. They say the beautiful Indian princess Cateechee (or Issaqueena) rode ninety-six miles to warn her lover in the colonial settlement of an impending Cherokee attack. Most historians agree, however, that Ninety Six already had its name when this event supposedly occurred. Most likely Ninety Six received its name when a surveyor estimated, by riding his horse, that it was ninety-six miles to Keowee, a major trading post of the Cherokee nation. Ninety Six appears on George Hunter's survey map in 1730 (now in the Library of Congress) and on the first recorded plat, that of Thomas Brown, in 1738. Brown chose a site where the Congaree and Savannah Town paths met "at a place commonly called and known by the name of Ninety Six." A second map adjoining this one was laid out in 1744 and described the area as "96 miles from the Cherokee Nation."

Besides the historical name, Ninety Six is home to the historical Star Fort. In 1760 the fort withstood a fierce attack by Cherokees losing their land to new settlers. (The peace treaty took all hunting rights away from the Cherokees and limited their movements to the north of Keowee.) During the American Revolution, Star Fort was an important British post. Many locals supported the crown as being more responsive to their need for law and order, but other colonists were just as adamant about the need for independence. In my youth the earthen fort was an open field where children played and teenagers got into mischief. Now the fort with its surrounding land is a national historic site, and a visitors' center describes the fort's creation and the significance of the battle of Ninety Six.

Another historic incident featured a native of Ninety Six. In 1856, as sectional differences over slavery were tearing the country apart, Edgefield congressman Preston Brooks, who had a large planation just outside the town, went onto the US Senate floor and with his cane pummeled abolitionist senator Charles Sumner of Massachusetts. Many white southerners thought the attack was justified because Sumner had given a speech insulting the state of South Carolina and personally insulting Brooks's kinsman, fellow senator Andrew Pickens Butler from Edgefield. At Ninety Six a grand dinner honored Brooks; the *New York Times* reported it to be the largest gathering ever in the upcountry, and Brooks received a wagon load of canes to replace the one he had destroyed assaulting Sumner. The event is commemorated on a plaque in the town center.

The war ended slavery, and during Reconstruction Ninety Six and the rest of South Carolina experimented with interracial democracy. African American men acquired the right to vote, and blacks as well as whites were elected to both state legislature and local government positions. One of the state's leading white Republicans, someone who worked for racial justice, was "Tieless" Joe Tolbert from Ninety Six. The majority of whites throughout the South, however, thought any step toward racial equality was intolerable, and the state government fell victim to a violent coup d'état that returned the government to white Democrats. One of the saddest episodes in state history was near Ninety Six: in the Phoenix riot in 1898 (Ninety Six native Dr. Benjamin E. Mays's first childhood memory), whites terrorized and killed an undetermined number of African Americans who tried to exercise their right to vote. The violence, intimidation, and murder continued sporadically for a year, until in August 1899 US Senator Ben Tillman spoke at the county seat of Greenwood, proffering to local whites to cease their "devilment" or the federal government might intervene. "If you want to uproot the snake and kill it," he urged, "go and kill the Tolberts," but be discriminating and "don't bother poor Negroes who have nothing to do with the Tolberts."

History marched on, and during the age of segregation, Ninety Six followed the Jim Crow pattern common throughout the South. Local textile mills were a whites-only enterprise. The segregation law was repealed in 1960, but separation of the races in textile mills continued until enforcement, or threat of enforcement, of the Civil Rights Act of 1964. When I turned sixteen, I got a wonderful job in "the shop" in Self Mills in Ninety Six. On the weekends the mill generally closed down, and I cleaned, painted, and did lots of maintenance. Oftentimes on the weekends, the only other folks in the mill were two or three African Americans who worked not in the mill but around it. Since there was only one bathroom, on those weekends we integrated the men's room.

In 1965, after I graduated, Ninety Six schools allowed some choice, and a few African American children began integration. One was Skip Williams, the younger brother of one of my best childhood friends, who entered the previously all-white Ninety Six High School. In 1971 the schools were fully integrated. After civil rights became the law of the land, Ninety Six came to an appreciation of all its citizens. In the 1970s Ninety

Ninety Six fountain. Photograph by Patrick Wright.

Six was one of the first towns to elect a woman mayor, Mary Bell, and with only about a twenty-percent African American population, the town elected Charlie Harts, an African American mayor in 1995.

Ninety Six has accepted modern life with gusto and satisfaction. It enjoys the amenities of small-town personableness and mirrors the best of the New South in its acceptance of civil rights. The Ninety Six School District educates its students in three well-integrated schools. People of all races smile and wave to each other when passing.

Today Ninety Six is very proud of its most illustrious citizen, Dr. Benjamin E. Mays. President of Morehouse College and spiritual mentor of Martin Luther King Jr., Mays was well known in the African American community and in the age of segregation almost unknown among whites. Ninety Six now has a monument to this apostle of peace, who gives us a different model than that of Preston Brooks.

This history has affected my love of Ninety Six in a very specific way, and that is the study of community. The community of Ninety Six was my world, and the First Baptist Church was the hub around which other activities revolved. With joy we attended every church activity: Sunday morning and evening services, choir practice, youth activities such as Sunbeams or Royal Ambassadors, and Wednesday night prayer meetings. My favorite hymn was "Jesus Loves the Little Children," with its message

Vera Human Burton. Photograph courtesy of the author.

that Jesus loved *all* children everywhere—"red and yellow, black and white, they are precious in his sight." The song echoed my mother's beliefs. Yet churches were segregated. As a religious child, I was perplexed about the animosity some whites felt toward African Americans. I wondered why the white people in my church did not want African Americans to attend, and that question, which led me into thinking about the history of race relations, still animates my research and writing.

Churches also reflected status and perhaps class, but my Ninety Six had no real aristocracy; there was no Episcopal church in the town. Social lines were not clear-cut, but few if any mill workers attended our "town" Baptist church, although quite a few farmers did. My mother often drove out into the country to bring others to church, and on one occasion there was some grumbling that the guests did not wear proper clothes.

Vera Human Burton seldom spoke out at church meetings, but when she did, people listened. This was one of those times, and the complaining ceased. I learned at an early age that conflict can characterize community and that chains of exploitation as well as ties of charity and cooperation could bind people in one. I saw that there was much that was not right with race, gender, and class. I realized firsthand the immorality of inequities in my hometown, and I learned to separate the people for whom I had affection from some of the things they did.

My life has been one of crossing boundaries—boundaries of race, geography, class, and status. I crossed the boundaries from Georgia to South Carolina, boundaries from southern, rural small town to northern, urban and university town, and back to rural Ninety Six. I crossed the boundaries from farm and working class to professional. In my work I crossed interdisciplinary boundaries, drawing on social sciences, literature, and quantitative and digital techniques. With my work in both history and computers, I crossed strict academic boundaries into public history, trying to democratize access to information and computers. I crossed boundaries from the classroom to the courtroom, where I worked with some of the greatest civil rights lawyers to fight segregation and to increase minority representation in government. I have been invited to cross two oceans to give talks on the South in Europe and Asia, and always I spoke about my hometown of Ninety Six. I have crossed so many boundaries that sometimes I am confused about where I belong.

But I do know where I am from. My parents came to Ninety Six as part of a white migration, looking for jobs as farming played out. South Carolina had industry, and relatives came to live with us while they found work in the cotton mill or power company. Two cousins stayed in the state, but most returned home to Georgia. I knew Ninety Six was rural, but my cousins from Georgia thought they came to the city when they visited. When we could get Granny Bess to visit, she refused to drink water from the faucet, sending me to the spring in the woods. (In an interesting departure from segregated race relations, African Americans and whites shared this spring and often got water at the same time.)

Mom sold insurance for the Nashville-based Life and Casualty Insurance Company. As she drove her insurance route out into the country collecting payments and visiting families, she would sometimes pile me in the 1954 Chevrolet with a load of books, and I would read for hours. My memories of visiting rural folks on their farms and in their homes are vivid. We often returned without being paid for the insurance premium, but we had a trunk full of garden produce, ham and sausages, and beef. Mom's insurance route also included the mill village, where she would park the car to save gas and walk from home to home. As a youngster I noticed the unfair treatment my mother received as a woman working in a man's world, and it filled me with anger.

Because my mother worked, I had what was euphemistically called a nurse, an African American woman who minded me, prepared meals, and helped with the housework. If my mother were still alive, I would never say that we were poor because she would vehemently deny it. But we had very little money. And yet we had an African American woman working for us. Even poor white families in the mill village had African American domestics working for them and caring for their children. It was a sad and unjust situation when working in the homes of unaffluent whites was one of the few economic opportunities for African American women. For African American men before enforcement of the 1964 Civil Rights Act, there was little job opportunity outside of manual and farm labor, unless they owned their own farms or businesses—and few did—serving African Americans as barbers or undertakers.

Something very important to me growing up in Ninety Six was my friendship with Charles Willis Williams; like everyone in his family, I called him "Brother." I was pretty naive; it took me a long time to know why some whites teased me about my "black brother." Our homes were near each other's, across an unsegregated cow pasture, and we ate meals together at each other's homes and had overnights together. Brother was a few years older than I was, and before I started school I went with him from time to time to the segregated, so-called colored school, where his mother, Mrs. Catherine Williams, taught. We were pretty much inseparable. Brother was better at everything than I was. When we boxed I always was the white guy that Joe Louis or Floyd Patterson beat up. In the miles of woods behind our homes, known as "Little Mountain," we had wonderful and dangerous adventures, one with an escaped convict, another with poisonous snakes. This interracial friendship was not in the least strange to me, and it continues to this day, though Brother and I live and work far apart. Having spent his life in the military, Brother retired and works in a veterans hospital in Albany, New York. He is looking for a place in Ninety Six to retire, and the two of us recently looked for places near mine on Lake Greenwood. Like me, he wants to have a place where he can garden.

From my African American friends, I learned other versions of history, other views of my community, and other people's motivations. Even more complex, I grew up with triple segregation; African Americans went to one school, white rural and town kids went to my school, and through the grammar school years, friends whose parents worked in the cotton mill, who lived in the "mill village," went to the mill school. I recognized early on the boundaries of class and place.

The complexities in this one community led to my work. In all of my writings on southern history, I try to capture a sense of mystery and

The author with George K. "Skip" Williams, left, and Charles Willis "Brother" Williams, right, 2012. Photograph by Georgeanne Burton.

contradiction and what C. Vann Woodward has described as the "irony of southern history": the legacy of slavery, the cultural combination of African and European roots, the peculiar quality of caste and clan, the enduring stereotypes, the ability under the most unpromising of circumstances to produce figures both black and white of literary rank, the persistence of gracious living and the aristocratic style, the distorted image of the southern politician, and the bitterness, violence, and hope of the civil rights movement.

Growing up in the rural farming, cotton-mill town of Ninety Six gave me a sense of being home, of living in a world where no one was a stranger. Like many rural places in America, Ninety Six has changed. Without the cotton mill, the town lacks the jobs it provided. Gone is the thriving community, vibrant with local retail and grocers, fresh meat and fish. I often caught that fish myself, in the Saluda River, farm ponds, and what we called Buzzard's Roost Lake—now Lake Greenwood—and sold it to those fish markets that day. Downtown Ninety Six in the early twenty-first century has mostly restaurants. Folks were thrilled when a Hardee's opened in town. Several restaurants of note include the longtime Cheeseburger House and the 96 Tire & Oil Company, which touts the "world's best hot dog." Symbolic of ethnic changes in the population, Ninety Six has

Mexican and Chinese restaurants. Now one of the largest employers is a Japanese firm, Fuji Film, which has a plant about five miles past where I grew up out in the country, on what used to be a cotton plantation, where one can still see a few of the pecan trees that used to lead to where the antebellum mansion stood. Even without its economic base, the town and its local churches promote community.

I feel humble about trying to capture the meaning of the South. When I write about southern history, I feel a kinship with my home community, black and white. I delight in southern hospitality and storytelling, but I hurt for my homeland's harsh treatment of minorities. I ache for the harmful myths we still believe and for our inability to face the truths about the past that shaped us and continues in so many ways. When people fly the Confederate flag, I think of Charleston native Harvey Gantt, who once explained that if you cannot appeal to the morals of a South Carolinian, you can appeal to his manners. Do we really want to injure the feelings of a group of people who have suffered so much in our state?

Ninety Six is less a place for me and more like my experience, my narrative—like a poem, my story. My place of the heart is intensely personal, it has often broken my heart, but this place and this story of Ninety Six has also at times inspired my heart and stirred my soul. As I sit at my desk in Ninety Six, writing and reading history, I marvel at the beauty of Lake Greenwood. As I watch a blue heron fly or the fish school, I know that I am happy to be home. And though home changes, we all change, and that is part of my story that I am telling even as I write today. ↄ

In Search of Peanut Butter Pie

My father was something of a troubleshooter for his company and thus was sent hither and yon to deal with problems and establish business for them. As a result, by the time I was eleven, we'd lived in six different houses in South Carolina and Tennessee. Finally my father said, "No more moving! We are here to stay."

"Here" was in Travelers Rest, South Carolina, a drowsy place with 1940s and '50s store-fronts, even though it was the early '70s by then. Travelers Rest sported fine places such as the Traveler's Restaurant, Brown's Feed and Seed, and Williams Hardware. When the Hardee's opened up, all of us teenagers thought there might actually be a Heaven on Earth. Fast food and rock and roll were the mantras by which we thrived. What did we know?

The progressive churches in town were Travelers Rest First Baptist and Travelers Rest United Methodist. If there were people who didn't attend church on Sunday morning, I didn't know about it then.

In Travelers Rest if you got into trouble on Monday, everybody knew about it by Tuesday, usually before your parents did. Of course, they found out in short order. There are no secrets in small towns. Travelers Rest High School was the home of the Devildogs, not to mention the school patronized by Furman University faculty and supporters. When I told my history teacher, Mrs. Moseley, that I had no clue where I'd go to college because my parents couldn't afford it, she informed me that I'd be attending Furman University, and she set out to make it happen. To quote Mrs. Moseley, "Well burr!"

In short, Travelers Rest was a nice place to grow up; a place where people cared.

Café at Williams Hardware. Photograph by Nancy Murphy Lance.

Fast forward a couple of years—to 2005, to be exact. Travelers Rest was a nice place to be *from*. Many of the places that made up the downtown area had closed, including Williams Hardware. Some forward-thinking planners in the city of Greenville started considering turning the old Swamp Rabbit Railroad into a bike and walking trail that would wind through the Greenville and Furman area and eventually end in Travelers Rest. It turned out to be a good idea. Around 2010 people started riding their bikes on the trail and stopping at vendors along the way.

Enter the McCarrell sisters. Joyce and Nancy were a few years ahead of me in school. Their father was one of three town doctors. Everybody knew him and, in turn, them. They called—still call—each other "Sister." Both of them were warm, intelligent, and willing to vocalize all those things that most of us were afraid to say out loud. This was a trait much admired by this shy young girl just entering her teens. I, and a lot of my friends, looked up to them.

As the story goes, somewhere around 2007, Joyce and Nancy decided that since Williams Hardware was right in front of where the Swamp Rabbit Trail was to run, that it was the perfect spot for people who might need a place to stop and eat lunch. That's when the Cafe at Williams Hardware got its start. The sisters purchased the property, and the restaurant opened

Sisters Nancy and Joyce McCarrell with their star attraction. Photograph by Nancy Murphy Lance.

toward the end of 2008. It was the first of many. Now Travelers Rest is the place to be.

This is where I come in. The Cafe is famous for its Reuben sandwich. I love the Reuben, but I have my own food lust going on. I can't pass the glassed-in dessert counter without going into spasms of sugar-coated, cream-filled desire. I gain three pounds just walking into the place, but it can't be helped.

My drug of choice is peanut butter pie. My love affair with peanut butter pie began with my first pregnancy in 1987. The Briar Patch, situated directly across from the video store where I held my second job, lured me in with promises of the cold, creamy pie. I craved it night and day. Since we had no money to speak of, I had to choose my guilty pleasures carefully. I chose peanut butter pie. I'm surprised Cathy, our firstborn, didn't arrive needing a peanut butter fix.

Here's the thing. I got over the pregnancy, but never the craving. Yes, I can make peanut butter pie, but my husband won't touch it, so I'd end up eating the whole thing. That's why I was so thrilled to hear it calling me from the dessert counter at the Cafe. "Melinda . . . oh Melinda . . . I know you can hear me!" Loud and clear. When it gets to the table, it is laced with

The Wednesday regulars, from left: Nancy Murphy Lance; Melinda Long and her mother, Alpha Brown; and Nancy's mother, Linda Sims. Photograph by Nancy Murphy Lance

chocolate and caramel syrup. This is what heaven tastes like. Somebody up there loves me.

Every Wednesday I pick up my mother, who still lives just outside of "T.R.," and we meet friends at the Cafe. Linda Sims, my second mama during high school, and her daughter Nancy Murphy Lance, my dear friend and one-time basketball teammate, meet us there. We sit down on the back porch if it's warm, inside if it's not. Mama and I share bacon and spinach quiche, the Rueben, or whatever the special happens to be. Nancy and her mama share, too. If we're feeling skinny, we all share a dessert. You already know my favorite, but I allow for Nancy to have her red velvet cake and Linda, her coconut. I mean, if you have to twist my arm, I'll eat a few bites. Ahem.

All of us talk old times, like basketball, band, and high school days, old friends from T.R., books, and whatever news is worth tossing around. We invariably run into locals we've known most of our lives and not-so-locals we've known for shorter times. The waitresses call us by name and fuss if we don't make it on any given Wednesday. Joyce and/or Nancy McCarrell always welcome us with a hug and "How are y'all doin'?" Later they make it around to tell us about what's happening, both good and bad. They suffered with me (and laughed at my hobble) through my broken leg. They rejoiced with my son's college graduation and my daughter's wedding. Basically, it's home.

In search of the perfect peanut butter pie? I know where you can find it and some nice conversation to go alongside. Travelers Rest, South Carolina, is now the place to be in the upstate, but, I'd like to point out, I knew that a long time ago. ☽

Seven Children Pose for the Camera, Sandy Island. Photograph by Bayard Wooten. Courtesy of Brookgreen Gardens Library and Archives.

The More We Play Together

Beautiful Black Children: Photo 1930s

Do you wonder why they're smiling?
Do you play the games they play?
Are they on the way to school or back?
Would you like to know their names?

Are they too poor to buy new shoes,
or do their toes just love the dirt?
Are they classmates, friends, or cousins?
Do they share each other's hurts?

Can you imagine them talking to you,
if you listen with your heart?
Do you share their dreams and wishes?
Are they human? Are they art?

Do you think they're always smiling?
Do you think they love this place?
Or do they dream of flying
far, far, far away?

Dinah Johnson

☽

Getting Schooled

At eighty-seven, I have explored and experienced the many faces of South Carolina, most of them with a dog at my side. When asked to choose just one to write about as my favorite, it was tough to answer.

Today, I am playing Frisbee with my dog, Chaser, and we are at the large fountain pool that is the gateway to the college where I retired in 1996. Watching her race around the perimeter of the pool, I reflect on the water and ponder how to decide on one that is the most of many favorites. As Chaser rounds the pool, jumping for her Frisbee, it becomes obvious. Wofford College.

But I need to back up a bit to explain. I need to back up a lot.

I was born a Depression baby in Memphis, Tennessee, rich in southern culture and character. We didn't have a lot of material possessions and found comfort through hard times in the camaraderie of the church. In the thick, syrupy days of summer, my mother would send me to my Aunt Lillian's farm in rural Mississippi, where it was my obligation to attend Bible school at the Church of Christ. During the summer of 1945, when I had just turned seventeen, I was sitting in the third pew on the last Sunday after a full three weeks of Bible school. My legs were so sweaty they were clinging to the seat, and I was secretly rejoicing as I daydreamed about swimming in the lake to cool off. It was during this moment that I found Pastor Waylan James smiling broadly and speaking directly to me in front of the entire congregation. I just caught the end of what he was saying. He finished with "Am I right, J.W.?" I had become somewhat of a teacher's pet with Pastor James these past few weeks with my outspoken curiosity of the Bible and Christianity.

Too embarrassed to admit that I had no idea what he was right about, I leapt into an over enthusiastic agreement: "Oh yes sir, yes sir, I do believe you are absolutely correct!"

"Praise the lord!" was his response, and the congregation cheered with equally enthusiastic "Amens!" After the service Pastor James came up to congratulate me with a huge bear hug. Apparently I had committed myself to following in his footsteps to become a man of God. Oh Lord.

Partly out of embarrassment and partly out of faith, I began my journey as a seminary student. The next four years found me on the lush campus of Abilene Christian College in Texas for my BA, followed by special studies in theology at Pepperdine University in California. I finished up my graduate work with a master of divinity degree at Princeton Seminary and became an ordained Presbyterian minister. I was heavily drawn to the Ivy League schools. They excited me with their tradition, beauty, and, most important, passion for knowledge.

It was at Princeton where I met the love of my life. Sally has been my partner and best friend for sixty years. And it was Sally who encouraged me to take the leap out of the ministry after six years to follow my bliss and go back to graduate school at the University of Memphis, where I received my PhD in behavioral psychology. This winding road led me to my teaching position at Wofford College in Spartanburg.

I was captivated by the beautiful southern campus as well as the challenging academic regimen. This combination of beauty and scholastic excellence has garnered Wofford the label of the "Harvard of the South." It was the perfect place to call home.

Most of the 1970s was filled with a rich academic life at Wofford, where I continued my laboratory research with rats and pigeons. This environment supported my passion for discovery. It was in the early 1980s, inspired by my dog Yasha, that I made the switch to using dogs as our subjects in the classroom. Yasha was a border collie mix with a flair for learning new behaviors very quickly. He also was fearless and became my companion everywhere I would go, be it kayaking, hiking, or swimming. So it made perfect sense that he would accompany me into the classroom. He exceeded my wildest expectations and not just as a research subject but as my full-fledged teaching assistant. If my students didn't discover something new about learning with Yasha, it wasn't because of any lack of capacity on his part.

Yasha became a bit of a celebrity on the Wofford campus and even garnered his own faculty ID. The entire staff and student body embraced and supported my four-legged friend. Unfortunately I was never able to achieve my goal of teaching Yasha proper nouns, although I highly suspected that it was my methods that were flawed.

When Yasha passed and I retired, I began struggling to find my place outside of the classroom. I puttered around with my windsurfing in Charleston and kayaking up on the Nantahala River but wasn't finding the spark that possessed me during my tenure at Wofford. I found myself becoming a frequent student in Bernie Dunlap's classes at Wofford and wandering through the faculty lunchroom to catch up on the latest activities, but I was seriously missing the engagement with students, missing my research, and missing playing with Yasha.

The only activity that remotely excited me were border collie exhibitions. During my teaching years, I would bring legendary border collie breeder and trainer Wayne West over to the campus to give demonstrations to my students. And now in my retirement, I would come home from Wayne's farm in Pauline, chattering endlessly to Sally about the incredible achievements of these dogs. She was becoming less and less enamored with my jabbering and hanging around the house. So it was Sally who finally snapped me out of my slump, informing me that I was getting a new puppy from Wayne's farm, and that dog was Chaser.

To say that this pup filled the void in my seventy-six-year-old life was an understatement. She became my child, my muse, my heart and inspiration. Her enthusiastic joy as well as her thirst for knowledge were matched only by my own.

During her early years of training, I once again found myself on the campus of Wofford College. This time the Wofford administration, students, and faculty were embracing my new four-legged friend, granting us an "all access" pass to the campus.

Our days begin around 5:30 A.M. at the Richardson Building. I have been given a key to the building so Chaser and I can arrive at this ungodly hour to work out before it opens. It's desolate when I begin my routine, and Chaser usually disappears to return with a blue ball that she has clearly stolen from the racquetball court. I toss it around the empty room and watch as it bounces off various equipment and mirrored walls as Chaser races to chase it, bringing it back to me as I am stretching. She takes a moment to imitate me in a bow and stretch with the ball in her mouth, then tosses it to me as she runs in the opposite direction. We repeat this ritual a few more times until the students slowly start to trickle in to take their place on the machines. Chaser greets each one with her entire body

Best friends on campus. Photograph by Mark Olencki. Courtesy of the authors.

wiggling, as if they are her long-lost friends. She really should try to play a little harder to get.

But she doesn't.

Today Chaser takes her blue ball to a brunette coed named Cat, who takes a few minutes of her precious workout time to play with Chaser. Cat is now on the treadmill with her earbuds in, focusing on her breathing, and I can see that she is trying to ignore the white-and-black dog intently staring at her with the blue ball in her mouth. Chaser tosses the ball near the machine and stares at the ball. No reaction. Chaser stares at Cat. No reaction. Chaser takes the ball back in her mouth and gently rolls it so that it comes to a slow stop at the base of the machine. She waits, stone-still in anticipation as Cat continues to ignore her, intent on finishing her workout.

I feel a little bad for Chaser, but not bad enough to intervene as I am enjoying the show. I'm wondering how long it will take for Cat to hop off the machine to throw the ball, but she doesn't, even though Chaser repeats this process two more times. I'm thinking it's about time for Chaser to coerce a new subject to play with her, but instead she takes the ball and carefully places it on the edge of the machine so that it is now within Cat's reach.

As she backs up, staring at the ball, preparing for the anticipated throw, I see Cat's mouth curving into a smile as she places one foot on each side of the machine to reach for the ball. Cat does this without missing a beat and tosses it across the room.

Victory! Chaser races after the ricocheting ball, dodging students as she lunges for it. She has managed to negotiate (or manipulate) the situation to her advantage. What other public space would permit me to bring Chaser, off-leash, to engage freely with others and witness her creative problem solving?

It is because of the limitless support of Wofford that I have achieved my success with Chaser. The Wofford community has granted me the freedom to think outside the box inside an environment that embraces discovery. And every time I enter the campus with Chaser—whether we are playing at the fountain, running through the great lawn in front of Old Main, working out in the Richardson Building, giving demonstrations in the McMillan Theater, or attending many of their sporting events—I feel like she does: happy in anticipation of seeing my old friends and making new ones. We are with our tribe. ☽

)

We Were Journalists Once. And Young

COLUMBIA, circa 1986—Unless you were winsomely young and in love and bursting with splendid plans, it was an unexceptional place. Just an ordinary swath of land, prone to neglect. But for me, it characterized a wholly magical time. And while it's not there anymore, having long been sacrificed to the dictates of progress, I visit it often in my memory.

Sundays were the only days I was keen to be awake and dressed by noon. Soon I'd drive my dented blue Saab, windows down, sunroof open, Crowded House blaring "Don't Dream It's Over," into the tiny parking lot next to an old ball field behind Dreher High School. It had humble aluminum bleachers, no dugouts. The grass was patchy and riddled with holes and fire ant mounds. It was perfect.

Soon my newspaper comrades would arrive slinging dusty bats over their shoulders and dragging coolers of cheap beer in aluminum cans with those old pull-tabs. This was our weekly pickup softball game. I don't even remember how it started or when it ended exactly, but for a time it was great fun. It didn't matter who won; I don't remember keeping score.

Back then, our newspaper building abutted Williams-Brice Stadium, and legends like Tom McLean, Bobby Hitt, and Charlie Byars ruled the newsroom. The intoxicating scent of ink and newsprint hung in the air. A wrought-iron spiral staircase connected the newsroom above and the composing department below, where a team of folks manually pasted and cut columns of type with X-Acto knives as editors directed over their shoulders.

I was part of the small editorial page staff of the *Columbia Record,* our city's afternoon daily. I'd been fortunate to work with two of the best in the business—Katherine King and Kent Krell. They gave me my first professional writing experience. But big changes loomed. The *Record* soon would fold. Katherine would retire, Kent would join the editorial page staff of the *State,* and I'd be absorbed into the newsroom of the *State* to work as a copy editor.

I was exceedingly shy in the beginning. My most confident days always had been on the athletic field. I ran cross country and track and played softball throughout high school, even threw the discus and javelin at the University of South Carolina my freshman year in 1979. This informal pickup game behind Dreher let me bond with reporters whose fondness for outdoor sports made them somehow more approachable to me. Adept at the old rubber-band method to limber up a stiff catcher's mitt, I was on comfortable ground kicking around the red dirt of a softball diamond.

How I envied every one of our ragtag group. They were witty, good-humored, and had been assigned special "beats," such as government, education, the arts, business, or health care. I longed to have a beat of my own.

It was the first time I felt like an actual grown-up. I had attained this job and chosen these friends all on my own (with no help from my out-going older brother this time). I treasured my nine-hundred-square-foot apartment down the road. It may have smelled like sulfur and stale cigarette smoke, but it was all mine. I loved that I could have beer and cookie dough for dinner if I wanted. Complete freedom.

One Sunday before the game, as we were tossing softballs around, warming up, the sound of crunching gravel caught my attention. A dark blue Buick Celebrity was rolling to a stop behind the field's chain-link-fence backstop. A white-faced Irish setter poked its head out of the passenger-side window. The driver—a lanky young man in sweatpants and a T-shirt, wearing a red bandana on his head—was Jeff Miller, the *State's* Newberry bureau chief. (They had bureaus back then.) The boxy Celebrity was Jeff's company car. (Yes, they had those back then, too.) He was unapologetically late. And I was immediately, unabashedly smitten.

Forgive me, gentle reader. (I've always wanted to say that.) I know the memory of an old flame unconsciously can muscle its way to the forefront of a story. Suffice it to say that I found Jeff to be dazzlingly handsome and enticingly aloof. The fact that he had a dog, Jeri, put him over the top in my book. Still, my memories come through the rose-colored glasses of young love.

Our group included newspaper staffers Debra-Lynn Bledsoe and Steve Hook (they would announce their engagement at one of our games),

Charlie and Janet Pope, Bill Robinson, Linda Shrieves, Tim Goheen, Steve Smith, Scott Johnson, John Battieger, Beverly Simmons, and Dave Moniz. People came and went from our game, and there are too many not mentioned here.

As our clique grew closer, in addition to playing softball, we had casual dinner parties, watched football or basketball games on television, took ski trips, took in local bands, and enjoyed libations at old haunts like Yesterdays and Rockaway's Athletic Club (the old one, before the fire).

Because a good number of us didn't have family in town, we began an annual orphan's Thanksgiving party. That evolved into additional themed "orphan" gatherings for other observances. Our parties were inspired and deliciously raucous. One of my favorites was the "Find the Lindbergh Baby" soiree, during which—properly fortified with our preferred beverages—we fanned out across the Shandon neighborhood for hours in search of a preplanted Lindbergh baby doll. I think there was a small kitty for the winner, but that really didn't matter. It was all about the chase.

In 2014 I contacted several of these old friends on Facebook to glean some of their memories. It turns out I was not alone in my affection for those days.

"Those Sunday afternoons made me feel a little less homesick," wrote former feature writer Linda Shrieves, who went on to spend twenty-two years as a reporter for the *Orlando Sentinel*. "It was a good and glorious time. Few responsibilities, other than deadlines. The life!"

Debra-Lynn Bledsoe, who married Steve Hook in 1988 and began writing a column, "Bringing Up Mommy," when she was pregnant with her first child, went on to see her columns syndicated by McClatchy Newspapers. She confesses a secret aversion to cowhide. "I screamed when the ball even looked like it might need to land in my glove!" But, she added, "those were the best days of my life."

Today, Debra-Lynn and Steve live in Kent, Ohio, where Steve is a political science professor at Kent State University and author of multiple publications on US foreign policy and diplomacy. Debra-Lynn is a professional photographer, blogger, and syndicated family-life columnist. They have three children.

"In all the moves Steve and I have made over the years, we have never found a cohort of friends like we had with you all," Debra-Lynn wrote her former colleagues on Facebook. "All these many years later, we are still trying to find what we had at the *State*. For me, it's not so much nostalgia for youth. It's journalists. They are a different animal. Curious, interested, open and eager to learn all there is—whether we're in our twenties like we were then or our fifties like I think we all now are. . . . You all were more than colleagues. . . . You all were the best friends of my life."

Even Jeff Miller, the hapless recipient of my long-ago affections, weighed in. "We were just kids," he said. "I loved those games. They were competitive but in a fun way. And it was great—especially when I was new to South Carolina and living in Newberry—to come into the big city and get to play with friends." These days, Jeff is a communications executive with a major nonprofit civil rights organization based in Washington, DC.

"In hindsight, I can see that the ball field was another kind of field— where we were nurtured by our environment and primed to grow," said Beverly Simmons Shelley, now a marketing director at the South Carolina Department of Parks, Recreation, and Tourism. "It's all kind of a haze to me. Did we really live that sweet, carefree time? It was our own field of dreams!"

I left the paper in 1989—defected to the "glamorous" world of nonprofit communications, which paid more and had better hours. I never was assigned a beat. In the years since, I alternated between nonprofit communications and journalism jobs. At one point I became a magazine editor (my dream job). In 2012 I published a modest book of poetry and got involved writing for local arts magazines. I still work in nonprofit communications. It has been a circuitous journey, but I didn't do too badly. And I'm still plugging.

Eventually the echo of those aluminum bats faded. Before the field was razed in 2005 to make way for the expansion of Dreher High School, I sometimes returned to sit alone in the empty bleachers, breathe deeply, and reflect. It's always game seven, and the most important pitch is the next one. ☽

Charleston artist Elizabeth O'Neill Verner. Photograph from the Collections of the South Carolina Historical Society, Charleston.

Charleston

"That was what has always puzzled me; we all, every one of us, see a different Charleston and yet we are all in accord on this one point. There is no place like it in all the world!"

Elizabeth O'Neill Verner (1883–1979), in *Mellowed by Time: A Charleston Notebook*

My Charleston Is a Movie Set

Two Charlestons rise up in memory when I recall our thirty-two years as residents of South Carolina. One is the familiar city of history, fine restaurants, carriage rides, the cannonade that touched off the Civil War. The other appears behind a scrim of memory, showing images from the location shoot for the *North and South* miniseries in the 1980s—two twelve-hour shows of a kind no longer feasible in today's television market.

But producer David L. Wolper had a lot of clout in those days. Indeed, the head of ABC had recommended my novel to David, virtually a gold-plated commitment that nevertheless took eighteen months from option to the first day's shooting—this, I don't doubt, to arrange for the go-ahead on a reported sixty-million budget for the first twelve hours.

At the time my wife and I were living on Hilton Head Island, basically an enclave for retired Yankee vice presidents a hundred miles south of the Holy City. We visited the *N&S* location six or seven times during the long shoot; the shows were filmed back to back. Scenes appear from that forgotten time:

I see Patrick Swayze, young and handsome, dashing from spectator to spectator around the set following each take: "How did I do? Was that all right?" On one such occasion, having been assured he did well, he planted a kiss on the cheek of our youngest daughter, Victoria. She will never forget; indeed I wonder if she washed that cheek for days afterward.

By contrast Patrick's costar, James Read, never seemed to need or seek reassurance. He tended to disappear from the set when the director called *cut*. James was a studious sort whom I never got to know well—likable, professional, but quiet.

The invading film crew was lodged at the old Francis Marion Hotel, just up King Street from the historic district. Here too were the production offices, spotted along the ramshackle corridors of the aging hostelry. I remember a communal room that may have been on the top floor (or not), where members of the cast gathered to roister at ten or eleven at night after a long day of setups around the town. David Wolper, a classy guy with a silvery beard and a mild demeanor (except when he was angry) met nightly with members of his staff in the not-very-good restaurant of the hotel. This group included David's son Mark, who now heads the organization passed on when David died.

The director of the pictures was Richard T. Heffron (d. 2007), a veteran of TV and movies, a middle-aged balding man who rose around five in the morning to get ready for the day's work. He must have been exhausted by nightfall, but he showed up in the communal room with a bottle of champagne from which he slugged a drink from time to time. I was later told that he carried a wad of bills to finance the drug habits of certain members of the cast. Being an outsider, I never saw any evidence of it.

One set-up in particular aroused the local media—a street overlooking the Battery, freshly sanded for the filming. There a miffed local resident insisted on parking her Mercedes to protest the intrusion. Dick Heffron foiled the spoilsport, whom I always imagined to be a Yankee move-in, of which Charleston has a lot, by planting artificial greens to block the camera's view of the car.

Charleston landmarks not only represented the antebellum South but its opposite number, Lehigh Station, Pennsylvania, where the Hazard family hung out. An historic mansion on Meeting Street was used for those scenes, with horsemen passing out front and James Read and company emoting inside.

Sometimes the morning's call required actors and crew to be on the road north of the city, to Boone Hall, a handsome stand-in for the fictional Mont Royal plantation, complete with a broad avenue of arching trees Patrick Swayze galloped under going to or from his fictional home. Here we sometimes saw the older but still lovely Jean Simmons, Patrick's mother in the picture, enjoying her canvas-backed chair on the sidelines—enjoying a cigarette, too. David Carradine was there, ready to swan around as the villainous husband of Madeline Fabray (Lesley-Anne Down) before Orry Main, her real love, took her away.

The grind of picture-making over a period of five or six months proved an incubator of romance. In 1988 James Read married Wendy Kilbourne,

Holy City close-up at First Baptist Church. Photograph courtesy of the South Carolina Film Commission.

who played his romantic interest in the story. Genie Francis (Brett Main) married actor-director Jonathan Frakes, and that union too has survived, along with Lesley-Anne's marriage (her third) to the DP on the second twelve hours. Terri Garber, playing the fetching Ashton Main, married a member of the crew, but it didn't take. I can't testify to what must have been any number of additional liaisons common to actors working out of town.

It was a magic time for me, and never more so than when the line producer, Paul Freeman, asked my wife, Rachel, to do a small, nonspeaking cameo at the conclusion of the first twelve hours. Paul became a good friend and was a relative of a fellow I'd worked with in Dayton, at the local office of Dancer Fitzgerald Sample, a New York advertising agency. Cynical old me knew that Rachel was jobbed into the picture to keep the book's author happy, as indeed it did. She was nervous about the request, but I urged her to go ahead, and she did. Ever since she has dined out on her morning in the makeup trailer parked outside the hotel, seated between Morgan Fairchild and Genie Francis.

Rachel's role was Mary Todd Lincoln, descending the lobby stairs of the Mills House on the arm of Hal Holbrook, who had spent a couple of hours in the makeup chair getting ready to portray her husband. Kindly but firmly, he told her where to stand (to his left—he "took the camera" in order to dominate the scene). I liked Holbrook; indeed I was too filled with starry adulation to dislike any of the men and women I met. The staircase descent in the Mills House was handily completed on a dismal rainy morning; a local actor playing President Buchanan languished in a carriage out in front and, as I recall, did not get much if any screen time. Rachel's presence is still quite visible in the picture, for which I'm grateful.

There was a great to-do when Elizabeth Taylor came to town. David had gotten her to play the madam of an elegant brothel. She was perfectly prepared for her one scene, filmed amid a great crush inside a house belonging to the College of Charleston. Ms. Taylor was late to the set and, I was told, received her usual emolument—jewelry, I think—in addition to her salary.

The mob crowded into that house was alarmingly eager to see the star. Rachel and I were shoved aside by a PR lady who didn't realize we had connections to the production. Later I got a chance to say hello briefly to Ms. Taylor, and to gaze into those aging but still lovely lavender eyes. I got an apology from the PR lady too.

On every visit we would stay two or three days, then drive home to Hilton Head, where I was working on the next book. Always the cast and crew were in my thoughts, and the West Coast publicity chief, the late Bob Wright, who became a good friend, kept me apprised of activity in Charleston. When the film was nearing completion, Bob arranged a press tour that brought news writers from all over the country to the set for interviews and general merry-making. We had a fine dinner at a local restaurant and a boat trip out to Fort Sumter, where I chatted up ABC's then-vice president of miniseries, Christie Welker.

Then it was all over, and the traveling circus moved on to locations in Natchez and elsewhere. I was later reunited with Wolper and some of his actors when ABC held a press preview of the show in Los Angeles. I was urged to talk favorably about the production, which wasn't hard. I was later telephoned by the late Brandon Stoddard of ABC, who liked what I said. Well, better that than the other way.

Charleston remains the shining centerpiece of those days. Networks no longer can afford lavish outlays for shows such as *North and South,* but I'm grateful they did back then. The experience filled me with wonderful memories of a Charleston that no longer exists except on film.

Author's Notes

North and South remains the seventh-highest-rated miniseries of all time. It debuted at a time when the three major networks virtually controlled TV content, before the proliferation of cable networks began offering a greater diversity of programming.

David L. Wolper began his distinguished producing career as a maker of documentaries, which he sold station by station until his track record was established. He is noted for producing the miniseries *Roots* and *The Thorn Birds*. Later he expanded into major films such as *L.A. Confidential*. Near the end of the location work in Charleston, the state government awarded him the Order of the Palmetto.

Because of the press of time, a second production team led by Robert Papazian developed the second twelve-hour show, known as *North and South II*. Many changes introduced in the story line did not spring from the novels. *North and South III* (a.k.a. *Heaven and Hell*) aired in the 1990s and was deemed inferior to the two blockbusters preceding it. The three pictures have never lost their fan base and are shown together around the world every year. ⟩

Safe Keeping

I call my father, who is originally from the Philippines, and ask him what he remembers of Charleston, the city where I was born. In particular I want to know about the events surrounding that morning in the hospital of Saint Francis Xavier, the first Catholic one of its kind in the state. Being both a poet and memoirist, I'm interested in any story he will offer about my childhood, but here's the truest thing I can say about this tendency: I just like hearing my father's voice.

He speaks to me in English, the accent from his native Tagalog still present in his speech, even though he has been living in the United States for more than fifty years. I take comfort in this evidence that the islands have not left him entirely, that some experiences, ones of which we might not even be aware, would graft to us, would envelop us with the binding husk of memory.

I've heard my father tell stories about his childhood in the province of Nueva Ecija, am happy to hear them, but there is one specific story that haunts me, even now. It involves his helping my grandfather harvest rice, *palay*. My father, so small at the time, had fallen near the throat of the threshing machine meant to free the grains and, having been pulled along the conveyor belt, was jolted in the shorn heaps destined to be crushed. He screamed. It was my grandfather, whose name I carry within my own name—*Marcelino*—who lifted my young father away and saved him and, in turn, saved me.

My father laughs when I ask if there were nuns present, since it was a Catholic hospital, after all, and he says, "Yes, yes, they wore those . . . what do you call them?"

"Habits?" I say.

"Yes, *habits*. Yes, that's right."

I imagine these women with their long garments, the clenched hems sweeping along polished floors of long corridors. In the story of my birth, the nuns hover in the periphery, and my father enters the hospital and carries with him the traces of a recent dilemma. In those early morning hours, my father couldn't find a babysitter for my older sisters, who were at the time six and four years old. So he made a spot for them in the backseat of our family's blue Ford Fairlane and then told them not to open the doors for anyone. He would lock them inside. He remembers they were smiling.

His mind, understandably, is not on the city. It is also too early to see the light that will fracture endlessly on the nearby Ashley and Cooper Rivers. It is too early to account for the statuesque palmettos that, in daytime, punctuate the architecture like exotic, molting birds displayed on stands.

As an adult I have since returned to the city. I have admired it alongside other tourists, gazed on the fort pressed into the wash of the South Channel's static, and have ridden, through a sun shower, on a horse-drawn carriage with my own young family.

"We didn't know what we were having," my father says, laughing. "We didn't know because of how it was back then."

Back then.

I muse on the double stress, the spondee, this way of trapping history in language. I know my father means the limited technology at the time. It would be some years before the widespread use of ultrasound, before the appearance of those monochromatic snapshots of fetuses resembling baby dolphins or clustered tulip bulbs exploding slowly on a screen, confounding expectant parents everywhere.

Because my father was enlisted in the Navy, he was eventually transferred, and just like that, the landscape our family inhabited shifted two states north, to Norfolk, Virginia, a city equally wedged by surrounding waters and an array of bridges. Though pulled from the city, I often thought of Charleston. It became for me an otherness, to which I was inextricably connected. When my mother describes the summer of her pregnancy with me, she likes to mention the heat of the lowcountry, her own North Carolina accent coming through as she reminisces, and that her fingers were always sticky from the ripe mangoes my father brought home from the commissary. Even now I can't eat this fruit without thinking, oddly enough, of Charleston.

When my wife sends away for my birth certificate, so that we can have our important papers all in one place, we're surprised to discover the paperwork contains an amendment. My father's middle name, *Tiangco,* had been recorded incorrectly. I imagine the attending nun, the folds of cloth and shadows draped, her head tilted above the desk as she listened intently to my father excitedly spelling out the letters of his mother's maiden name: *Ti-ang-co.* Somewhere down the corridor I am barely audible, and in this imagining, I believe he hears me, his infant son.

The old façade of the hospital, at least the version of it in my father's story, has vanished into walls of sunlight. Blocks away are the brushed and shiny uniforms of the Citadel cadets who stride swiftly on downtown sidewalks while their parents follow a few steps behind, prideful of their children's transformation into adulthood. There are still the dried palmetto leaves feathering and falling while, in the distance, the bridges to Daniel Island and to James Island traverse rivers where the boats are purled and anchored, their sails folded and stowed away for safekeeping. And within the brightness that is this city is another light, a faint one. This light rests above the parking space my father had found. It falls over a car where two girls are locked away, because it was safe *back then.* I'm told my sisters said a prayer for our mother to please have a boy. I'm told that in this moment they were safe, all of them, the family I soon joined, and the city held them, as it holds me still. ☽

The Precipice of the World

Early in 1979 our parents announced that the family was moving to Charleston from New York City. We were eight and ten years old, and our experience of Charleston was limited to several visits to family friends who lived well out of town on Seabrook Island, a place that to shut-in kids from graffiti-encrusted, Son of Sam–haunted New York was so fabulous and so fun we could barely believe it existed. There was a video-game arcade just steps from an Olympic-sized swimming pool with diving boards! You could ride horses and sail boats and swim and fish and drive a golf cart all in the same day!

So we imagined we were headed to this sun-splashed, suburban dream-life where, on top of it all, we'd build a skateboard ramp in the driveway and hang a backboard and a net from a two-car garage. When we landed, then, in *downtown* Charleston (a place we'd never even visited), we were shocked to learn the home we'd be moving into—a tall, yellow 1789 townhouse on Rainbow Row—not only was miles and miles from our resort-town idyll, but also would accommodate neither skateboard ramp nor basketball hoop. What was worse, the house smelled terrible—like mushrooms and dirty clothes. It hadn't been lived in for several years. There were many tears and days of sulking, and our parents enlisted us in de-mildewing the place, wiping down every painted surface with Soft Scrub–soaked sponges and paper towels.

To be fair, Mom and Dad tried their best to comfort us, with trips to the Hungry Lion on Broad Street for mustard-slathered cheeseburgers and cold glass bottles of Coke—a drink they hadn't permitted back in Manhattan. Our mom walked us to the East Bay Playground, a block away, and introduced us to Hazel V. Parker, the kind woman who presided over it from a pavilion on East Bay Street where she sold ice pops and candy bars. Hazel showed us the playground's tennis and basketball courts and the baseball diamond. We could, in fact, monitor the goings-on in the outfield from our third-floor bedroom window!

But even more than that, there was freedom—something we'd never experienced in New York. We had permission to explore this microcosm on our own, without our parents' supervision, and it was exhilarating. At first we weren't courageous enough to go much farther than a few blocks' radius from the house, but it felt exotic and wondrous nonetheless. We rode our BMX bikes down South Adgers Wharf to the railing-less granite pier where fishermen cast their poles and tossed chicken necks on a string into the murky harbor to reel in blue crabs. There was a dock parallel to the pier where gray boats with the word *PILOT* in bright orange letters along their hulls were tied up. Our dad had told us that this was the pilot boathouse and that the captains of the huge tanker ships we saw coming into the port of Charleston from all over the globe would call the pilot at all hours of the day and night for assistance. The pilots would then get in their speedy gray boats and drive to meet the tankers at the mouth of the harbor and guide them into the port docks off Morrison Drive to unload. True enough, from our beds we could hear the diesel engines of pilot boats thrum to life at all hours of the night.

Pretty soon we forgot about the arcade games and swimming pools of Seabrook. We joined the baseball league at the playground and spent countless afternoons with friends, riding our bikes around our new world. And as we grew older, the city's appeal only deepened. By the time Matt had his driver's license, at age fifteen (fifteen! in our New York friends' minds, this was scandalous!), even the parking lot on South Adgers, in front of the playground—which had never held much allure for us— became the place where we'd spend afternoons waxing and working on the old car our uncle had given us. In history class we learned that South Adgers Wharf was the terminus for the first New York-to-Charleston steamship route, and that fact seemed to speak to us uniquely—showing that despite the apparent cultural differences between the two cities (which we were becoming more and more aware of as young adults), there was a deep and enduring connection between them. We'd find ourselves walking down South Adgers Wharf to the granite pier whenever we were on the verge of leaving Charleston—on high-school trips and returning to college from vacations. There was a feeling of standing at the precipice of the world that was at the same time comforting and exciting.

South Adgers Wharf. Photograph by Brandon Coffey.

The docks. The playground. The parking lot. This small world off East Bay Street was the start of Charleston's way into our hearts, the beginning of half a lifetime's worth of the Holy City and the Palmetto State working their magic on us in so many ways. In our careers as cookbook authors and travel writers, we're constantly asked how we got where we did. And the simplest answer is to say: *We grew up in Charleston!* But that answer—which might be intuitive to a Charlestonian—only seems to invite more questions, about what that means. We find that whenever we can, we take visitors back to our corner of the world, to the pier on South Adgers.

There have been a few changes since our BMXing days. The pier has been made into a feature of the beautiful Waterfront Park, but everything's pretty much the same: the pier has no perimeter fence or railing, the parking lot's still there, and so is the outfield of the Hazel V. Parker (RIP) Playground.

And it still, more than anything, has the power to communicate to visitors the powerful effect this city can have on you. Something about standing on the pier overlooking the harbor, asking visitors to imagine being eight or ten years old, crystallizes for them so much about how our hearts ended up here. They see the 420 sailboats and the tankers in the harbor. They listen to the burble and swish of the tide against the pilings. Gulls circle overhead. A neighbor's walking her dog in the outfield. Two pilots are uncleating the lines of their boat. With all the senses, you're overwhelmed by how much standing on this small pier, in this small city, can make you feel like the world's at your doorstep. ☽

Sutherland-Masters House in Pickens County. Watercolor by Marjorie Schaefer. Courtesy of the artist.

Better Homes and Gardens

This Old House

The Sutherland-Masters House was deep into its second century when "discovered" by a young sightseer, some sixty years ago, on its twisty little road in the Blue Ridge of northern Pickens County. Enchanted by its setting—a garden spot of old hollyhocks, roses, and quince bushes backed by cornfields that climbed the lower slope of Table Rock Mountain—and its unpainted grace, with a blow-through breeze wafting white organdy curtains through its screenless windows, the visitor never forgot.

In 2000 that memory enticed a group of elderly writers looking for a retreat site to buy the forlorn former stagecoach inn. At that point abandoned, vandalized, and forest-reclaimed, it is now being lovingly restored as the office and studios of the nonprofit Birchwood Center for Arts and Folklife.

There's a sweet mountain wind once again blowing good.

Dot Jackson (1932–2016), the enchanted visitor who returned to the Sutherland-Masters House in later years and became the first director of the Birchwood Center for Arts and Folklife

Martha R. Severens

)

Better than the Real Thing

In November 1992, when I accepted the position of curator at the Greenville County Museum of Art, I sublet a studio apartment on Main Street across from the Hyatt. Unlike today, there were few residences downtown. I had moved from Portland, Maine, where I had been the curator at the Portland Museum of Art and my husband, Kenneth, taught in the New England studies program at the University of Southern Maine. We were trying to sell our 1840s Victorian row house there, and I was not supposed to go house hunting; however, I could not resist after noticing a listing for a "Frank Lloyd Wright–inspired house." In the early 1970s, Ken, an architectural historian, had done research on the great American architect in connection with a house in Oberlin, Ohio, where we were living and teaching at the time. We had traipsed all over the country to see Wright buildings—even landing in Greenville. I can remember standing on West Avondale Drive and staring down at an expansive roof; not much else was visible from the street.

When it came to buying homes, our goal was always to find something architecturally distinguished. After a decade renting uninspired apartments, in 1980 we bought a magnificent Greek Revival home at 2 Wragg Square in Charleston. Governor William Aiken had built it in 1845 as a rental property on a corner lot diagonally across from his own mansion. One of seven identical houses, it was large (4,200 square feet) and demanding, with insufficient heating and cooling. But we loved it nevertheless; Ken had a wonderful garden and even learned to grow okra at the request of our backyard neighbor. Four spacious downstairs rooms, somewhat inadequately furnished, were fantastic for entertaining, but the best place was the second-floor piazza, where we ate many warm-weather meals overlooking an avenue of live oaks. Both the property in Charleston and the row house in Portland satisfied our requirement for distinctive residences, but in moving to Greenville we were unsure what we might find. We were pleasantly surprised.

In 1951 Charley and Gabrielle Austin—two spinster librarians—decided to build a house designed by Wright on a three-acre lot just off stylish North Main Street, Greenville. The Austins visited Wright at Taliesin, his compound in Spring Green, Wisconsin, and he agreed to work with them. Although he never came to the upstate, he had been to South Carolina during the late 1930s when he developed Auldbrass, an extensive complex of structures for Leigh Stevens near Yemassee. The result was a modern plantation with a low-slung profile and decorative features inspired by Spanish moss. We had visited Auldbrass shortly after we moved to Charleston in May 1976; Ken was to teach that fall at the College of Charleston, and soon after I joined the staff at the Gibbes Museum of Art. Interestingly Auldbrass was the first lowcountry plantation we saw, well before going to the more traditional Ashley River plantations Drayton Hall and Middleton Place. In Yemassee we were the guests of Jessica and Stan Loring; she was the daughter of Stevens, and they were heroically trying to reclaim the property after decades of use as a hunting lodge.

The Austin sisters' home, known as Broad Margin, is an example of the Usonian type, created by Wright to address America's need for inexpensive housing. He invented the term *Usonian* as a reference to the United States of North America. His hope was that these structures would be thoroughly American, modest, and easy to build and maintain, but Wright being Wright and something of an idealist, things did not always work out that way. "The Usonian house aims to be a *natural* performance, one that is integral to the site, the environment, to the life of its inhabitants, integral with the nature of materials," he explained in his book *The Natural House.* "Into this new integrity, once there, those who live in it will take root and grow." By 1954, when he wrote this description, Wright had designed more than one hundred Usonian homes.

The Austin sisters were delighted with Wright's plans but encountered some difficulty finding a contractor willing to take on the assignment. They discovered their solution in Harold Newton, a young Clemson University graduate who not only took the job but embraced it. He worked with officials to ensure the design met local ordinances and with Nils Schweizer, an apprentice of Wright's who visited several times to lend assistance. The result is an intimate gem of residential architecture. With a sweeping roof, it nestles into the site, faces a creek, and turns its back to the neighborhood. The interior boasts many Wrightian features: built-in furniture, radiant heating under terracotta-colored concrete floors, a long hallway, clerestory windows, and a dominant fireplace constructed of concrete with inset boulders. In addition to the great room, it has three bedrooms and a very small "workspace"—Wright's term for the kitchen.

For Newton the experience was transformative; in 1975 he designed and built his own version of Broad Margin on a one-acre lot about a mile away. According to legend he did this without the knowledge of his wife, and although the Newtons lived in their house for seventeen years, purportedly she was never captivated by it. Perhaps as a concession to her—or southern middle-class taste—the house on Mohawk Drive has formal living and dining rooms, just the kind of spaces Wright had eliminated. These rooms are equipped with wall-to-wall carpet, full-length drapes, and white walls, all of which Newton had renewed before our purchase. Although we rarely use these elegant spaces, they are an ideal place for our eclectic collection of furniture and architectural prints reflecting Ken's interests: medieval churches, Charleston, Dublin monuments, and two aerial views, one of Portland and the other of Bellows Falls, Vermont, his birthplace. Newton also provided for a spacious two-car garage—anathema to Wright, who believed in carports. It's a great place for our VW Jetta and our extensive assemblage of wheelbarrows, lawnmowers, garden tools, and more.

Another concession to convenience is a stupendous kitchen, easily twice the size of the one at Broad Margin and equipped with two walk-in pantries and generous counter space. Newton definitely improved upon Wright's concept of the workspace. Its spaciousness is enhanced by a raised skylight, which admits a soft light and resounds with raindrops. The kitchen's best feature is the way it interacts with the great room on the back side of the house, allowing me never to feel trapped while preparing meals.

Raised two steps above the kitchen and entry level, the great room's walls and ceiling are tidewater cypress paneling with some of the most beautiful abstract patterns, illuminated by indirect lighting and daylight through narrow clerestory windows. A focal point is the fireplace, another essay in texture and design resulting from large rocks set into concrete. A lengthy built-in sofa provides a great space to sit by the fire, read, or stretch out for a nap. Probably my favorite space in the house, I love it best early on a sunny winter morning when the raking sun comes through the clerestory windows and bathes the wood and the fireplace.

The house on Mohawk Drive. Photograph by Russell I. Fries.

The cypress paneling continues down a long, narrow hall equipped with bookshelves and closets—ideal for two eggheads and packrats! Two modest-sized bedrooms open off the corridor; one we use as an office, the other as a den. At the far end is the master bedroom, with cypress walls and a peaked ceiling that reflects the slope of the roof.

When I first moved in on May 1, 1993, I began to live a Spartan existence—I borrowed two chairs and a six-inch-thick piece of foam and slept on the floor. Built-in desks and bureaus made this lifestyle very feasible and enjoyable until furniture and other possessions arrived five months later. And for fifteen months I was without a car, so I walked the mile and a half to the museum. It was a charmed existence.

The exterior with its handsome horizontal profile delights me whenever I return home. Set into an incline, the house is removed from the street, and a rock-articulated concrete base and entranceway make it all the more imposing. The overhanging roofline emphasizes and unifies the outside and allows for natural environmental controls: the interior is protected from scorching summer sun, but in the winter the low rays penetrate and warm the rooms that face west and south. It is, in the tradition of Wright, such a natural solution.

The house has been a source of inspiration and has fostered my research and writing and encouraged me to cook healthy and tasty meals. Now that I am retired, I have even more time to enjoy its many beautiful and practical features, somewhat relieved that it is less of a work of art than Broad Margin. Instead it is a livable and comfortable home, a delightful synthesis of artistry, creature comforts, and Wrightian functionalism. And as he prophesized, I have taken root and grown. ☽

A Garden Is for Re-creation

Almost from the time I could walk, I was involved with gardening. While I cannot remember quite that far back, there are family photos showing me "helping" my paternal grandfather in the yard. He employed a yardman for the heavy work, but everything within the flowerbeds was his territory.

Why did I spend so much time with him there? I'm sure part of it was because my "Big Dad" was a storyteller. To Ernest Edgar Sr., gardening was more than landscaping. Gardening was a story; plants had names and stories behind them, and he never ceased to be in awe of watching a seed mature into a blooming flower. No matter how hot or miserable it got, he always seemed to be happy in his garden. And while he didn't talk to the animals, he did talk to his plants.

It was from him that I learned the names of plants; that good gardeners, especially southern gardeners, "passed along" cuttings or seeds from their most treasured plants; and that gardens are never-ending, always changing, sometimes mysterious endeavors.

Before modern gardeners began talking about "microclimates," he explained, sometimes through actual demonstration, that some plants needed sun and some preferred shade. I recall once that a neighbor did some rather severe trimming of trees along our property line, resulting in the harsh western sun hitting a bed of ferns. "Gotta move 'em," he said, "otherwise they'll be burned to toast in August." When I asked why, he explained about how our neighbor's tree trimming had changed what could grow in the once-shaded bed. He then moved all but one plant to a new location and passed along others. The one he left—as he had predicted —succumbed to the searing heat of a Mobile summer.

That lesson actually had two parts, because he pointed out that the neighbors had "butchered" their trees and shrubs. One tree died because it had been cut too far back. And since the trimming had been in the late fall, it took several years for their azaleas to recover and bloom. Trimming trees and shrubs was not taboo, but when and how one did the trimming was important. Big Dad really preferred to let most shrubs "take their own shape." The oleanders and oakleaf hydrangeas reached the second story, the azalea bushes were ten to twelve feet in diameter, and I cannot remember his ever trimming our twenty-to-thirty-foot crape myrtle trees.

There were no fancy garden stores in those days with flats of ready-to-plant annuals or perennials. Instead he regularly visited the neighborhood hardware store, where he purchased seeds. Even when a few local nurseries began to offer some bedding plants, he insisted that growing your own from seed produced healthier flowers. Depending upon the season, some seeds went directly into the ground; others, including morning glories, were soaked in water before planting. Once the soil was broken and tilled in the beds, he would ask me to help him plant, then cover the seeds. Neat rows, each identified with an empty seed packet on a stick, soon filled the garden. Once the plants were up, there was always weeding. It seemed like there was weeding to do every day! "Whenever you come out to the garden, pull up the weeds you see," Big Dad would say. "Don't wait until they take over!"

My Big Dad died in 1954, but the lessons he taught me have remained with me for six decades. I have always needed to have dirt under my fingernails wherever I have lived, even if it only was a pot on a window ledge. Otherwise I just didn't feel complete. It was 1972 before I finally purchased the first and only urban real estate I would ever own. Over the next forty-plus years, I used much of what I learned about gardening from Big Dad to shape what is truly my own special place, my yard in Columbia.

The place on Hollywood Drive is not big by today's suburban standards, a 60-by-150-foot lot, but it was typical for a 1920s Columbia subdivision. By the time the footprint of the house (built in 1954), a two-car garage, and ribbons of concrete for an entry walk and driveway were subtracted from potential landscaping, I had less than 7,000 square feet and four different microclimates with which to work. The front yard was a southern exposure, partially shaded by a large mature elm, one of the last remaining ones that had once lined all of the streets in the Hollywood neighborhood. The east side of the house, a narrow nine-foot strip between the house and the property line, was shaded by a neighbor's house, a smaller elm, and a loquat. The ribbon drive took up most of the western side of the property, from the street to the garage. In the backyard there were three huge hackberries, two spindly pines, and two sad dogwoods. What passed for lawn was mostly centipede thickly sprinkled with crabgrass, dandelions, artichoke weed, and stickers.

In the front yard, the shrubbery looked like an architect's drawing, or larger-than-life pieces from a Lionel train set. The walk was lined with candytuft. A row of untrimmed American boxwoods stretched from the front door to the corner of the house, where loomed a large Burford holly. From there a thick patch of nandina grew down the west side of the house to the back door. Along the eastern property line were two mature eight-foot camellias ("Pink Perfection" and "Governor Mouton"). In the backyard the shrubbery consisted of a large mock orange, a single camellia ("Professor Sargent"), and numerous Carolina cherry laurels of various sizes and shapes. Between the driveway and the property line was a mass of liriope and weeds; between the driveway and the house, a narrow band of weeds.

When my late father-in-law, Harry Giles, came to see what Betty and I had purchased, his first comment was "Son, you need a bush axe and some weed killer." Those items and an electric hedge clipper were among his housewarming gifts. Since we intended to redo the house with sweat equity, landscaping was not high on my priority list. With Father's assistance, I trimmed the shrubs below the windows, thinned out the cherry laurels, began a three-year battle to eliminate the mock orange, and mowed the grass.

Now just because the house was my main concern did not mean that I simply became a twice-a-month lawn mower. We had hardly moved in when friends and our new neighbors began to bring us housewarming gifts of pass-along plants. One elderly lady brought us "ivy from Woodrow Wilson's birthplace" in Staunton, Virginia. As a southerner she knew how much I'd appreciate that, and she insisted she help me plant it along our neighbor's fence on the east side of the property. Another brought two oak-leaf hydrangeas. Other neighbors gave us scilla, Star of Bethlehem, daisies, and Helleborus. A rented rototiller helped us move most of the liriope in the backyard to the street, leaving open space for these new plants.

A few months after we moved in, my father announced he was selling our old family home in Mobile. A quick trip down and I returned with rice paper plants and a sack full of monkey grass. And my aunt said we certainly should have some horsetail and papyrus (which she called "Moses in the bulrushes").

There was no garden plan in those years. Just getting the gifts in the ground and keeping them alive was all. And that would be true for how we used the yard over the next twenty years. Daughters Eliza and Amelia came along in the mid-1970s. Our front lawn was open, and neighborhood children played there all the time. And after the elm fell victim to Dutch elm disease, there was a lot more space. A swing set in the backyard and later a basketball goal meant that whatever was going into the ground back there had to be pretty hardy. An addition to the house of another room and a screened porch led to more shrinking of the back lawn.

There was still, however, some space for a cut flower bed. I grew marigolds and zinnias from seed. For chrysanthemums I ordered bare-root stock from Park Seed. It was not a big bed, but with some TLC it produced more than a dozen blue ribbons at the South Carolina State Fair. Then I got lazy. I was no longer interested in competing at the fair. (Originally I had done so after being challenged: "Can't you grow some just as pretty, Daddy?")

By the early 1980s and a decade of just putting things in the ground, I began to develop a plan. Camellias had always been among my favorite plants. However, they are a natural understory shrub and like some shade. I contacted Bobby Green in Fairhope, Alabama, whose nursery specialized in heritage camellias, and described my yard. In the shade east of the house, all of the original shrubbery went and was replaced by camellias. They have thrived there ever since.

The removal of the elm in the front yard had created a sunny microclimate. After a trip to Charleston and the purchase of some "popcorn berries," my girls asked if we could get a "popcorn tree." I checked with some botanist colleagues, who assured me it was a fast grower. And it was. Eventually that tree and one of its scions would turn the front yard into the shade garden it is today.

After the girls went off to college, the borders in the backyard expanded, and in went more camellias intermixed with varieties of oakleaf hydrangeas. Interspersed were a few hardy perennials. I was looking for pretty much a low-maintenance yard. With two cars and street traffic increasing, a circular driveway in the front obviated the need for a lawn. If I wanted seasonal color, a flat or two of something from a big-box store sufficed. Betty's declining health and what seemed like an ever-busier professional life left little time to work in the yard. I sold my lawn mower and hired a

The author with one of his grown-from-seed zinnias, now six feet tall. Photograph by Allen Anderson.

yard service. In essence, by the early part of this century, I had a yard, but I'm not sure Big Dad would have considered me a real gardener.

Then Nela entered my life. After we decided to get married, we went through the process of deciding where to live. Her house on Bancroft Court? My house on Hollywood Drive? Sell both and start anew? One of the things she said to me after we had spent a day on Hollywood Drive was "Your garden is an expression of you. I bet there are lots of stories here. Let's talk about it."

And then I did. About the pass-along plants that were still in the yard: oakleaf hydrangeas, Helleborus, scilla, papyrus, and horsetail. Who passed those along? Nela asked. Well Myrtis Singleton gave us the Helleborus and scilla, Julian Kennedy the star of Bethlehem, Inez Watson the oakleaf hydrangeas, and Margaret Rembert the daisies. The Woodrow Wilson ivy from Emily Bellinger Reynolds almost took over the tree house I'd built my daughters in the huge hackberry in the 1980s. Eliza and Amelia said it was "roachy," so I got rid of it—a decision Nela wholeheartedly approved when I told her. Garden failures: I cannot grow tea roses. The plants that were too big for a small space: a glorious Cherokee rose, a fig tree, and a Confederate rose. The microclimate change when one big hackberry came down and too much sun killed a twenty-year-old oakleaf hydrangea. The rice paper plant from Mobile, now ten feet tall and providing afternoon shade for the screen porch; the sack full of monkey grass that now bordered every bed in the yard. The special camellias—some from Mobile ("Lady Hume's Blush," "Fashionata," and "Bessie Bellingrath"), the one from Betty's grandmother's homeplace ("Lady Clare"), and the ones that Flo and Tabb Heyward recommended I add to the yard ("Julia France" and "Magnolia Flora").

Nela has a particular love for azaleas. They were not in bloom, and since one azalea looks pretty much like another, she asked what they were. Under the limbs of the popcorn tree and among its tangle of roots, native azaleas flourished along with the colorful indicas I remembered from my youth: the watermelon-pink Pride of Mobile, the snow-white Mrs. G. G. Gerbing, the lavender-throated white Fostoria, and the deep purple Formosa—Nela's all-time favorite, as it turned out.

"It sounds as if almost every plant has a story," Nela concluded. "Walter, we can build or buy a new house. You cannot replace this wonderful garden you have been creating and re-creating over the past thirty-five years." So the decision was made to remodel the house on Hollywood Drive but keep the garden and work in it together.

Little did we know that we would face major changes over the next seven years. The original remodeling in 2007 made a mess of all the flowerbeds adjacent to the house and disrupted the irrigation system—the repair of which tore up the back lawn. A spring microburst in 2011 resulted in the taking down of two damaged pines and another large hackberry. A new addition to the house, our Edisto Room with glass on three sides, and the removal of a utility pole and burial of all utility lines were, I hope, the last time there will be major destruction in our garden.

In re-creating the garden after each of these challenges, we have thought in terms of what we would like to enjoy not just from being in the yard but from our screened porch, the dining room, our studies, and the Edisto Room. As we worked on the garden, the old tradition of pass-along plants continued. Nela added a yucca from her house at Edisto Island—the scion of a plant from her great-grandfather's house—and our friend Eleanor Pope gave us tiger lily plants that were descended from plants Nela's mother had given her. But for a while we were simply purchasing flats of bedding plants. Then in the summer of 2014, on a lark at my favorite little hardware store (ACE Hardware in Cayce), I bought packets of seeds (nasturtium, zinnia, marigold, morning glory, moonflower). It was a little late for some of them, but WOW, did they ever produce. They thrived and provided color and cut flowers until frost, while the store-bought plants struggled. Watching the moonflower tremble and open in the moonlight was as magical as I had remembered it to be. It was so exciting I asked neighbors with children to come over and watch.

When I was asked to write this piece for *State of the Heart,* I knew I'd choose my garden, where almost every plant has a history, a story to tell. The garden I now cherish and tend also tells a story of passing needs and tastes, of miserable failures and some celebrated success. Do I talk to my plants? Yes, just like my grandfather did. I've found that nothing will spur a drooping specimen to perk up more than the threat of uprooting and tossing it on the mulch pile. And I smile and give thanks for moonflowers. Like us all, gardens and gardeners grow and change over time. In retrospect I was just as happy with having the sunny neighborhood playground as I now am with a shade garden and heritage camellias.

Big Dad was right. Gardening was his recreation, but with each new season and every pass-along plant, he re-created something special—something in his heart, and mine. ☽

Anthony DuPre and Ted Barrett in Jeremy Creek, McClellanville, 1940s. Photograph courtesy of the Village Museum, McClellanville.

Children, Water

The Boat

All things worth the knowing
They claim a river knows.
And where it's worth the going
Is where a river goes.
Oh, to be that boy.
Oh, to bail a boat.
Oh, to be that boy
And once more be afloat.

William Baldwin, *Village Lives and Other Poems*

Once More to Campbell's Pond

For a day that had started with so much promise, not a lot was going right. My dad had dropped me off with our johnboat, a paddle, and a floating seat cushion for my first-ever solo fishing expedition. I was going to catch a largemouth bass that day, and the only question in my mind was how big it would be.

By midmorning, however, I had managed to get tangled with every underwater snag in the pond, and now my favorite minnow-mimicking lure—a red-and-white Cisco Kid—was hopelessly embedded in my shirt.

I was twelve years old, still naive enough to think that fishing trips were supposed to turn out like the articles I read in *Field & Stream* magazine. Maybe you read them, too, the epic tales of anglers who always outsmarted those wily "lunker mouth" bass.

It wasn't impossible to catch a big bass here. This was Campbell's Pond in Manchester State Forest, the same pond where my sister's husband had caught a 10-pound 2-ounce largemouth just a few weeks before. The fish was already stuffed and mounted on their wall, and now Campbell's Pond had become my mecca, beckoning me to come and catch my own lunker mouth.

I didn't know it at that tender age—though numerous fishing trips in the years ahead would make it plain enough—but the fishing gods had already decreed who would and who would not catch big bass. I was destined to catch other things, like branches in trees.

Not twenty minutes after I had removed the last treble hook of the Cisco Kid from my T-shirt, I managed to cast the same lure smack dab into an oak tree overhanging the dam. The Kid dangled down from a limb, its artificial mouth grinning at my folly. Tugging and pulling on the line wouldn't bring it down, but I had paid three dollars of hard-earned grass-mowing wages for the darned thing. I wasn't about to leave it hanging in a tree.

So I paddled to shore, shimmied a few feet up the trunk, and started sawing through the branch with the serrated blade of a knock-off Swiss Army knife. The unwieldy device had a spoon, a fork, a corkscrew, and a dozen other useless implements. The saw blade wasn't dull, just out-matched for the task of gnawing through the two-inch branch.

But never underestimate the determination of a skinflint adolescent who wasn't about to give up on his lure. An hour later, the branch had finally succumbed to my efforts, and the Cisco Kid was back in the boat.

I was hot, sweaty, and worn out from lumberjacking, but it was still a glorious summer day, and I was fishing on Campbell's Pond. The twelve-acre pond was so long that, with its bend in the middle, you couldn't see from one end to the other. Like any optimistic fisherman, I knew there was a bass, a big one, waiting for me to cast in just the right spot and—whammo!—I, too, would join the ranks of those *Field & Stream* anglers.

After a makeshift lunch of canned sardines and soda crackers, I decided to give the Cisco Kid a rest and try another lure. I still can't figure out why I did what I did next.

I clipped the line to tie on a different bait, but absentmindedly didn't notice that the tip of the rod was hanging over the water, not the boat. Gravity did its work, and the Kid hit the pond. I watched as the unteth-ered lure faded into the murk as if in slow motion. Only when it vanished did it dawn on me that my favorite lure, the same one I had rescued time and again that day, was now irretrievably gone.

I would return to Campbell's Pond many times, eventually driving myself to Sumter County from Columbia in my dad's truck. Though always stingy in giving up fish, the pond had become a familiar friend. There was something reassuring about fishing in that green-black water, surrounded by endless trees.

My dad retired from his career as a forester a few years later, and I didn't go back to the pond for a long, long time. In fact it was several years after he passed away in 1999 that I saw it again. I discovered it had been drained for dam repair, and a five-year drought had kept the pond from refilling completely. Nearly half of the basin was empty; cattails grew up in the now-dry ground at the shallow end. It felt strange, like seeing a long-lost friend and being embarrassed about their gray hair and wrinkles.

Campbell's Pond. Photograph courtesy of the author.

But then something even stranger happened. I returned to Campbell's Pond in the past few months to show a friend, and it was as if time had reversed course. Several seasons of normal rainfall had refilled the banks. The pond of my youth was back.

Standing on the dam near the overflow pipe—the same place where my brother-in-law had caught his big bass—I looked out toward the far end and smiled at the pond's familiar bend. I was once again surrounded by forest, the same one my dad had helped to tend.

This was where he had allowed a twelve-year-old to venture out on a boat alone, a day in which that adolescent version of myself first began to connect the dots that a fishing trip is almost never pure joy. In the more than forty years since, I've found there's often a little misery mixed in: a lost lure, a motor that doesn't start, an anchor rope that won't hold. You just have to muddle through the bad parts and soak up the good parts, wherever they can be found. ◡

Black Water River

You can smell it before you see it—wet earth, rotting leaves, and something else, something fresh. Something alive. The Edisto River breathes its way leisurely through my hometown of Orangeburg on its way to the sea at Edisto Island.

The longest unobstructed blackwater river in North America, it was a beckoning presence in my early life. I learned to swim in cold, sun-dappled shallows where the water was the color of tea. We called this shallow place "Rocky Bottom." Here my cousins and I played on black inner tubes that became so hot in the sun you had to keep turning them over in the water to cool them off.

I remember hanging out the window of a car filled with kids and inner tubes when I was little and feeling sorry for all the other people in other cars who weren't going to the river. When we got there, Mama would sit in the shade under veils of Spanish moss with my aunts and other ladies while my sisters and my cousins and I made a mad dash for the water. It was always a shock. The Edisto River is cold, even on the hottest summer day.

After the initial icy plunge, we swam underwater and dog-paddled on the surface. My cousin Jim taught me that it was okay to open my eyes underwater. His father, my Uncle Herman, was one person among many who "taught" Mama to swim by throwing her into the river as a youngster. She became a very strong swimmer because Herman would make her laugh while she was trying to stay afloat; you have to develop some real water skills to be able to laugh while fighting the Edisto River.

Many kids my age were taught to swim at the river by Mrs. Mutch, a local lady who wore Rose Marie Reid bathing suits and high heels. I didn't

Edisto waterwheel. Oil painting by Kate Salley Palmer.

take lessons from her, but many of my contemporaries won lifesaving certificates at her direction.

We kids tried not to get out of the water to talk to Mama too often. We didn't want her to say, "Your lips are blue," and thus make us pack it in for the day. Sometimes she made us eat pimento cheese sandwiches and then sit with her for a half hour so we wouldn't get a cramp.

Downstream from Rocky Bottom was a main swimming area where teenagers frolicked on barrels strung on a thick wire along the bank. Big kids also dived off a dock anchored farther from the shore. As we got older and bolder, we outgrew Rocky Bottom and struck out for the dock ourselves. The river current was slow but strong, and you had to be a pretty good swimmer to make it. Mrs. Mutch made all her lifesaving students swim back and forth to that dock. I felt powerful and strong every time I climbed aboard. We knew that if we missed the dock, the only thing to catch us would be the net stretched under an old green footbridge that spanned a narrow section of the river below the main swimming area.

That old bowstring bridge is still there, its net still stretching bank to bank, straining the heavy current for washed-away valuables and people.

A day on the Edisto River, 1950s. Photograph from the collection of Dr. Gene Atkinson.

I know the bridge is really old, because my mother told me, after I grew up, that she used to dive off the top of its green arches high over the water. Mama, an athlete and daredevil in her youth, said the river was narrower and swifter then, and Rocky Bottom didn't even exist.

Diving from the bridge was prohibited by the time I was old enough to consider it, but most of the teenage boys my age did it anyway. At least they claimed they did.

The river narrows as it passes under the bridge, and tall cypresses on the banks compete with tupelo, willow, and other trees to reach out over the water. Lazy snakes coil themselves in the moss-shadowed branches, occasionally plopping heavily into the hull of a boat gliding below.

Downstream from the bridge are the Edisto Gardens, where more moss-draped trees guard huge azalea bushes along a path above the river. An old waterwheel still turns in the current near the rose garden. I painted a picture of that waterwheel when I was fourteen. It was my chosen subject for informal art lessons taught by a neighbor of ours at the time. The teacher said I did "everything wrong, but it came out right." Mama kept this oil painting the way she did much of the artwork I did as a youngster, and I still have it.

The rose garden is famous for its abundance, vigor, and variety—even inspiring the annual Orangeburg Festival of Roses that features many community activities, from foot races to art shows. But nobody I knew ever swam in the garden section of the river. The main swimming area lay upstream from the bridge and bustled with people when I was young. It featured a large lifeguard stand on the beach overlooking the area of water enclosed by that barrel-strung wire. A long series of steps cut into a hill that sloped from the beach to the River Pavilion, a grand white building perched high above. We called it, simply, "the Pavilion." The hill from the beach to the Pavilion was steep enough to tempt boys to try to run from its top to the water without scraping their faces in the grass or the sand. Not many of them made it.

In those days a jukebox at the Pavilion blared the hits—"Blueberry Hill," "Ain't That a Shame," "Young Love," and many other songs I still associate with swimming in the river. You could get frozen Milky Ways there and soft drinks. By the time I was in high school, many people I knew had stopped swimming at the Pavilion and had attached themselves to various private swimming pools around town. They deserted the public swimming area at the river for the same reason that many whites abandoned the public schools in the sixties. The civil rights era brought racial integration to places throughout the South, and whites in some towns even closed public swimming facilities and other recreation areas rather than share them.

If the Pavilion swimming area at Orangeburg ever closed for a significant period of time, I am unaware of it. I do know that by the early seventies, it was open and integrated.

Today no one, black or white, swims in the river at the Pavilion. The culprit now is pollution. DHEC closed the swimming area for good in the middle seventies due to waste-treatment discharge and farm runoff upstream. The old Pavilion building is now home to the Orangeburg County Fine Arts Center.

I am writing about a place that still exists, yet it doesn't. There's no comfortable "what became of it." The river still looks the same: dark, slow, and inviting. I hope that someday children will learn to swim there again. And I realize how very lucky I was as a privileged child to have had the opportunity to spend summer days at that special place on the Edisto and to go home wet, tired, and happy, smelling like the river itself. ↄ

)

Summers on Stevens Creek

The sun had been up for less than an hour, and it was already stifling hot on the ridge overlooking Stevens Creek. Summer days were always hot in the 1950s, but for my granddad's logging crew, there was work to be done despite the heat—pine trees to be felled for delivery to the pulp mill.

While Granddaddy Bridges gave instructions to his straw boss, I took the Pepsi bottle filled with coal oil and rubbed a healthy splash on my arms and the back of my neck to ward off the swarms of mosquitoes, careful to not get any on my face where sweat would carry it into my eyes. There were no commercial insect repellents in those days, so we used whatever was available to keep the ubiquitous pests at bay. The coal oil mixed with sweat made the bulging biceps of the logging crew glisten like dew on clover in the early morning light.

Modern mechanization had yet to arrive, so the pines had to be logged and cut into sections by hand. Two men with a crosscut saw brought the trees down, then moved on to the next tree, while two more with razor-edged axes lopped the limbs and hacked the trunks into nine- and ten-foot lengths to fit on the railcar waiting on a side track in the little community of Clarks Hill, where my grandparents lived.

Once he laid out the plan for logging that day, Granddaddy turned to me. "You ready to go fishing?" he asked. I nodded. I was always ready to go fishing in those days.

We left the crew hard at work and walked downstream on the western side of Stevens Creek. While we fished all along the banks up and down from the old steel bridge on County Road 88 two miles from Clarks Hill, our destination that day was a place Granddaddy called the "Dairy Hole." The Dairy Hole was a juncture in the creek where swift currents ran up

Stevens Creek. Photograph by Tom Poland.

against a rock bluff, then turned to the right to flow more leisurely downstream. The change in direction created a pool of nearly still water, and the years of hydraulic force had washed out a deep hole in front of the bluff. Catfish and other species gathered there to wait effortlessly for the creek to deliver their next meal.

On the way Granddaddy stopped to cut two long green poles from a canebrake, trimming the branches with his pocket knife. Once we reached our destination, he dug into his overalls pockets and produced two balls of string to tie on the poles for line. My granddaddy's faded blue overalls were a treasure trove of necessities for the day—everything he needed to go fishing could be found in his pockets. Besides the fishing line and pocket knife, he carried a small brown paper bag with hooks and twist-on lead sinkers. He carried two flat Prince Albert cans in the breast pockets—one filled with tobacco to roll cigarettes with and one empty, to be filled with the night crawlers we dug from the creek banks.

My job was to bring the paper sack with our lunch: two RC Colas, some slices of Colonial Bakery white bread wrapped in wax paper, a small jar of Duke's mayonnaise, a small shaker of salt and black pepper mixed, and two ripe Marglobe tomatoes picked from Granddaddy's backyard garden that morning before we left. All that was needed to turn that into lunch was his ever-handy pocketknife.

For a youngster just reaching his teens, Stevens Creek was a wonderful place to spend summer days. And the Dairy Hole was an idyllic spot to sit in the shade of branches hanging from creek-bank trees for a fresh tomato sandwich with my granddad. To nature lovers—and scientists—the creek is a wonderful, if enigmatic, place to this day. Running along the border between McCormick and Edgefield Counties, the creek stretches a couple dozen miles from where it merges with Turkey Creek near Plum Branch to its confluence with the Savannah River near North Augusta. Except in the very lowest reaches, navigation is limited to paddlers, because shallow shoals and fallen logs in many areas negate the use of motorized watercraft.

The trip downstream offers a panorama of scenery and changes in landscape, from deep gorges on the upper end with swift riffles and rocky shoals remindful of upper Piedmont rivers to meandering currents and long, sloping banks on the lower end more like the slower-moving streams in the lowcountry. The scenery undergoes a metamorphosis also as the creek moves steadily toward its destination with the more robust Savannah—from steep banks lined with trees and plants more likely seen in the lower mountains of the upstate to shallow banks downstream lined with cypress knees reminiscent of lowcountry swamps.

If Stevens Creek itself is a near-hidden scenic wonder, then the bluff just above the bridge on County Road 88 near where my Granddaddy Bridges cut pine trees is the crown jewel in the setting. Here, from the crest of the bluff down to the swirling waters of the creek, is a plant community unlike any other in South Carolina, or in this part of the United States, for that matter, harboring at least fifteen rare plants, including some found nowhere else in the state. Scientists believe this unique array of rare plants and wildflowers hearkens all the way back to the last ice age.

Because the botany and geology of this region of Stevens Creek is so unusual, the Stevens Creek Heritage Preserve was created to protect its rare plants and animals. Managed by the South Carolina Department of Natural Resources, the 434-acre site features soil types more typical of Appalachian coves and the Midwest, and some of the plants, while rare in South Carolina, are plentiful in those areas. In writing about Stevens Creek, naturalist Patrick McMillan—faculty member in the College of Agriculture, Forestry, and Life Sciences at Clemson University, director of the South Carolina Botanical Garden, and the Emmy Award–winning host, cocreator, and writer of the ETV nature series *Expeditions with Patrick McMillan,* described the site as having a "combination of extraordinary color and rare species which can be seen nowhere else in the state."

The federally threatened Miccosukee gooseberry, for instance, is found in only two places in the world—this area in South Carolina and along Lake Miccosukee in the Florida Panhandle. Another peculiar species, Dutchman's breeches, is well known to northern botanists but in South Carolina is only found on Stevens Creek. While the woods along Stevens Creek are full of sedge species, the James Sedge, which is typical of limestone woods in the midwestern states, is found in South Carolina only on Stevens Creek. Visitors to the preserve are asked to stay on the 1.3-mile hiking trail to avoid trampling the rare plants.

As a youngster growing up in the late 1940s and early '50s, I knew nothing about the ecological uniqueness of Stevens Creek. I knew only that it was the most wonderful place in the world to spend a day fishing with my Granddaddy Bridges. ☽

Swept in with Her Tide

Feeling a slight chill slide down my arms was uncommon for early August in South Carolina. I grabbed a beach towel and wrapped it around my five-year-old. "No, Mommy," Mary said, slithering out of my embrace and reaching up for the breeze. "It feels good." The sun was just cresting the horizon as our family motored out for crabbing in the early morning low tide. Mary's two sisters, Margaret and Helen, were nestled up in the bow of the Boston whaler for a few last minutes of sleep during the short run to an isolated point on Harbor River, deep in the delta not far from the river's final destination at the Atlantic Ocean. Mary was clearly awake, alert, and immune to my cold-natured tendencies.

Sliding the towel around my own shoulders, I toyed with Mary's long blonde curls as the boat dodged the oyster rakes and threaded the narrow river, sucked exceptionally shallow by the full moon. The gray pluff mud shimmered with the rising sun. Our beloved Spring Island was rubbing its crusty eyes and beginning to stretch its arms for another hot summer day. The odd mullet jumped, breaking the sleek still of the water. A rising school of shrimp raced in circles just below the surface, causing a subtle flurry of disturbance and gaining the attention of a couple of seagulls. They swooped down and effortlessly plucked a couple of shrimp from the river for a quick breakfast.

As we glided past the green and gold marsh grass, a snowy egret took exception to our presence and modeled all of its five-foot, snowy-white wingspan as it lifted from its perch in the mud with slow, dramatic beats of its wings. It soared over our bow and headed into the blinding glare of the sun. Henry eased the engine. "Wake up, sleepyheads, and throw the anchor over," he yelled. "We're ready to crab."

Margaret, the oldest at eight, sleepily started pulling out the rope and chain for the anchor. Two-year-old Helen climbed out of her mound of towels and headed in a slight stupor to the basket containing the crab lines to make sure she procured her favorite three. A little too slow off my mark, I failed to keep Helen from hugging her treasure. Thus she, in her precious pink bathing suit, was now sticky with the juice of the baited chicken necks. Blue eyes glimmering beneath her veil of red curls, she grinned so hard her freckles stretched. No matter how happy and cute she looked, I had a mother's moral obligation to destroy the morning peace and dip her in the dark river to rinse out the chicken juice. The quiet morning was no more.

Henry threw the anchor just beyond the edge of the stranded marsh grass, looking much like an expert cowboy lassoing his steed. His three daughters proudly clapped and cheered. "Easily impressed!" Henry said, smirking as he jumped across coolers and baskets to help me divvy out the remaining crab lines and assign each daughter her allotted footage on both sides of the boat. Strict trespassing rules required that we avoid any crossing of property lines during the next several hours of crabbing.

The girls unfurled the weathered, light brown string entwined around thick sticks with chicken necks and small anchors tied at the end. With the water still shallow, only a short amount of string was needed for landing the chicken necks on the river bottom, where they enticed crabs returning on the incoming tide. I followed behind Henry's placement of each girl in her assigned space, smeared as much sunscreen as possible across their milky complexions, and topped three heads with hats.

As the girls peered over the sides, each taking a very serious account of any possible crab line vibration or water movement, there was a moment of complete calm. With the boat tucked in a small curve of the bank, a velvety heat started to descend and envelop us.

Helen let out a small gasp and yanked her line up so fast her slimy chicken neck flew across the boat, slapping Mary in the bare part of her back. "Got one!" Helen yelled.

"*Helen!*" Mary shrieked. "Gross." She dashed for the cooler to pour clean water down her back. "*Mom,* please help me!"

"Where the crab?" Helen said as she stumbled around, looking all over the floor for a large crab.

"*If* you did even have a crab on your line," Margaret said in a school-teacher tone, "you can't catch him by pulling the line up so fast. You must pull it up slowly, like this," and she reached down to demonstrate.

The author with her mother and daughters on their way to a post-crabbing float on Harbor River, 1998. Photograph by Henry Clay.

Henry picked up Helen and walked to her side of the boat. "Come on, tree frog, I'll help you. You just need to slow down your retrieve a bit, and you'll catch a big one. But first, say sorry to Mary."

"Sowwy," Helen mumbled, eyes downcast and slightly pouting as she watched Henry lower her line back into the river.

Fifteen slow minutes passed as the rising heat intensified the crabbers' impatience. The low tide sucked the life out of any potential breeze and convinced the water to be still as death. Even the marsh grass stood motionless, stranded on the slick mud flats left with no water from the ebb tide.

I understood our daughters' impatience because I remembered my own, crabbing as a child with my grandmother. I could almost hear her voice: *Be patient, Emily. Give the crabs time; they're coming.* Now, during our treasured vacation days on Spring Island, I could share the love of river life with our girls—if only they could hold on a few more minutes. After all, we had to give the crabs time.

Glistening with sweat, Margaret let out a whoop. "Dad, grab the net. I've got one!" She furrowed her brow as she inched up the lightweight line.

Inhaling a breath of thick air, Henry eased the crab net into the water without making a ripple and held it poised about a foot from the line. As Margaret pulled the string a tad higher, he swished the net under the bait and lifted out the first harvest of the day: two large blue crabs, each capable of conversion into a few ounces of tender, buttery meat. Henry dumped them into the thin wooden basket, robustly shaking loose the tight grip of the claws on the tattered, gray chicken necks. The two crabs turned on each other in the basket and, with great commotion, fought each other with their claws pinching wildly.

As the tide rose, the girls released more string to keep the bait on the river bottom, grabbing the attention of a steady march of crabs returning with the flow of the current. Over the next couple of hours, Henry and I kept busy between netting crabs and congratulating the jubilant crabbers. An occasional slight breeze offered welcome relief in the midst of the sporting frenzy. When several dozen warring crustaceans filled the basket, we convinced the girls to pull up the anchor and head back for a refreshing swim off the dock.

Harbor River, rushing to achieve its high tide, changed with our mood. We were finished with crabbing but not with the river. I dabbed the sweat once again beading on my forehead and anticipated the joy of plunging into the dark water for a delightful midday swim. The boat streaked around the bend, edging closer to the marsh grass as the water spread widely across our path. The breeze pushed the gray moss draped in pendulums in the large oaks overhanging the high bluff. The little girl in my heart wanted to hug Harbor River and thank her for continuing to woo me with her beauty and for entertaining me with endless pursuits. I'm really no different from the Atlantic blue crab. Both of us are swept in with her tide. ☽

James McBride Dabbs—farmer, professor, writer, and civil rights activist—in the study of his Rip Raps Plantation in Mayesville. Photograph by Ed Eckstein. Courtesy of the South Caroliniana Library, University of South Carolina, Columbia.

Land Rich

"It would be strange if I were not a Southerner. Sitting by this window, looking down the avenue along which I hurried as a boy and down which I have seen my children and grandchildren walking with their dogs running beside them, I feel the throb of this land in my blood."

James McBride Dabbs (1896–1970), from *The Southern Heritage*

Deep Country

Where to begin the tale of my favorite place in South Carolina? There are so many potential starting points that choosing one feels a bit like placing one's thumb at random on the wheel of time.

But perhaps it makes sense to begin where I enter the story, around a half-century ago, with memories of my father and mother, teachers on nine-month contracts in the segregated South Carolina schools of the 1960s—he the band director of the legendary "Fighting Cobras Marching Band" at North Charleston's Bonds-Wilson High School; she a teacher of English and math nearly forty minutes away at Haut Gap, a school serving the rural Gullah communities on Johns Island.

Marking the school year's end was a ritual we'd enact every June—as the final exams, final concert performances, and graduation exercises were checked one by one off to-do lists. Away would go my school uniforms, carefully pressed and packed in plastic and mothballs, into a trunk in the attic. Out would come the summer dresses, skorts, and playsets, the lightweight chinos and seersucker suits to be packed as carefully into suitcases. Out would come Dad's toolbox, for the hours of tinkering under the hood of our red 1960 Catalina—all unmistakable signs that soon we were to hit the road.

As he worked, I'd hover. "Where are we going, Daddy?" I'd ask in a singsong child's diction, though I knew perfectly well, so well my insides seemed to be spinning hula hoops in joyous anticipation.

"You mean you don't know, daughter?" He'd smile, well aware of his part in our play-acting. "We're going to D.C."

"D.C., Daddy? Like Washington, D.C.?" I'd say. Though again I knew perfectly well we weren't driving to the nation's capital, even though the president and Mommy's brother, my uncle and namesake, lived there.

"No, daughter dear, not the big city," Daddy would reply, chuckling his deep chuckle and poking my chest with a grease-stained finger. "We're going the other way, to the country, not the city. To D.C.: *Deeeeeep* Country."

I seem to recall that, the first time he offered this sally, it took me a full beat to get the joke. But every subsequent time, the tease leading up to the punch line would seem nearly to burst my heart with delight, and I'd laugh and bounce, and that hula hoop of expectancy would spin faster and faster and faster . . . until we had arrived at our destination.

Ninety Six.

Not the country town, one stoplight with a railroad crossing, a mill village, a few palatial homes, and a brickyard—not there, but the deep woods and farmland surrounding it, a tedious three-hour drive in those days down two-lane roads.

Deeeeeep country, home of my Mawmaw and Pawpaw—my mother's parents and all her kin—and their low, rambling. magical farmhouse built somewhere around the turn of the century with a spreading oak in front. Where water was pumped from a well and there were always flowers and sweet smells. Where there was a deep spring for swimming and fishing—and all manner of things you could eat straight from the woods: maypops, tart and orange; blackberries guarded by thorns and the occasional snake; wild plums; muscadines. And always the great call and response of the woods —bobwhites and wood thrushes, alternating with the lowing of cows and the braying of mules, days shattering with the buzz of cicadas, nights vibrant with frog song and the whistle of the whippoorwill.

I had a rich life in Charleston, my father's hometown, the place where I grew up. Things I loved included the rivers and the tiny excursion boat my father used to launch upon them, when he had the time; my school, Immaculate Conception, big as a cathedral and full of children of all colors, sizes, temperaments, ruled over by gentle African American nuns from the Order of the Oblate Sisters of Baltimore; my best friend's collie dog, who bore a striking resemblance to the one on television, though she had never once saved a kid who had fallen down a well. But I responded to none of these quite as I responded to Daddy's call of "deeeeeeep country." It was, has always been, the place my heart called home.

The story of how the town of Ninety Six got its name is epic, involving great sweeps of time, war, and the making of a people. But as a child my understanding was more properly that of a ballad—one of those great old-time classics such as "Fair and Tender Ladies," with dozens of alternating verses twanging the tune of star-crossed lovers, vows of blood vengeance, inevitable, tragic death.

This is the version I heard as a child.

Once upon a time there was an Indian maiden. Some said her name was Cateechee, the name, I later learned, of a river; others called her Issaqueena, the name, I also came to know, of a set of falls. Both geographical features were just north of Clemson, near Keowee, the largest of the towns on the Lower Cherokee Traders Path, now submerged under the waters of Lake Keowee, formed when the river was dammed in the late 1960s.

Of course I knew almost none of that then. What I knew was that this Indian girl (who at that time didn't even have a name) had a redcoat lover over at the fort. So great was her love and so hotly did her brothers object that they decided to attack the fort and slay not just the man she loved but as many of the settlers living beside the fort as they could to boot. Cateechee-Issaqueena, an intrepid lass, jumped on her mule (or stole a horse) and rode hell-for-leather for ninety miles until the mule dropped dead. Nowise daunted, she made the final six miles on foot, clawing her way through rocks and brush, first at a run, then staggering—finally crawling on hands and knees until she fell into her lover's arms, delivered the warning, then died. No one was particularly clear on why a six-mile run following a ninety-mile ride must be fatal, but one must admit it provided a great punch line to the story.

Now, even as a child, I knew there were holes. Though raised for the most part in the city, I knew enough of mules to know no mule alive could be worked until it would founder—they were way too smart, and too contrary, to bend to human will to their own harm. But everyone you'd ask would tell the story, word for word, the same way. Just like a ballad, its wildness cut up into bite-sized portions and made safe for children: a race war, whites against Indians, an unruly, transgressive love contained by the death of the desiring, dark woman. That was the tale of Ninety Six.

There was a dark, desiring woman at the heart of the story of how my family came to Ninety Six, too. But that story had to be pried from the cold pages of probate records and census forms, coaxed with great patience and much pleading from the shuttered lips of family members who, if not precisely sworn to secrecy, certainly behaved as if they had been.

The interest in roots among African American families has a specific date stamp. Before that date, trauma, shame, and forced habits of secrecy sealed many a lip. But fired in the 1970s by Alex Haley's book and the hit television series that followed, the study of roots took off. It has waned at certain periods and waxed at others, particularly now with a wave of technological advances: tools such as Ancestry.com and the Latter-Day Saints' Family-Search, which have simplified the task of digging for documents; DNA evidence, now able to be collected and analyzed at reasonable cost; and of course, television—series such as *History Detectives* and *Finding Your Roots*.

I've used the Internet extensively to fill in the blanks in my family tree. But the documents that tell the story of my family's origins and how they came to the land "down home" in Ninety Six were discovered by a previous generation of family sleuths, and they did it the old-fashioned way: with expenditure of shoe leather and acres of patience, turning the pages of old tax books and examining wills, city directories, and census books.

The critical piece of the puzzle in my family's case was one that never would have turned up online: an auction inventory from the estate of one James Richardson of Saluda, dated 1858, showing the purchase by his grandson "Jas. Hill" of three slaves: a "boy Abram," presumably a "prime hand" who went for the stratospheric price of $1,400; one "Becka," likely a child, who sold for only $475; and "Eliza and child," prized enough to sell, like Abram, for $1,400. (It should be noted that only three others on the entire "List of Negroes" parceled among Richardson's grandsons went for more than that price.)

While much substantiating evidence has been gathered over the subsequent years, this is the only document that exists definitively linking my great-great-great-great-grandparents: James Richardson Hill—a Saluda County planter famed for the excellence of his orchards, who later served as a private in the Civil War, indicating a late and perhaps less than willing entry into the contest—and Eliza, a woman whose presence in the historical record must mostly be inferred.

It was the children of this union, never blessed by marriage (though James Hill never married a woman of his own race, either), who found the land in the place we always called simply "down home": Fellie, the oldest, and his brother John, who "when peace declare'" and the great jubilee of Emancipation dawned, left Saluda to travel thirty miles to the north and west into Greenwood County.

There they found a white woman willing to sell land to newly emancipated slaves. They purchased adjoining tracts of fertile land watered by deep springs, more than one hundred acres of it for each of them, and along with another friend, one George Moss, who settled on a somewhat smaller tract nearby, they made their homes, fathering many children, planting at least two Baptist churches, Pine Pleasant and Pleasant Rock, and living the richly textured lives of country people who were close to the land.

My earliest memory of "down home" is of an event my mother tells me I could not have witnessed: a hog killing in early November.

"You were too young," she said to me a few years ago, in one of those long, rambling conversations we had about "the old days" shortly before she died. "We hadn't done one of those in years," she reiterated patiently.

But I could see it—see it now, so clearly in my mind. The frost twinkling like a fairy carpet of jewels in the weak wintry sun. The clothes I was wearing. The child's red wagon full of bloody bones I was dragging behind me in the fields. I recall that the grown-ups were very far away and very busy. And though there was the smell of blood in the air, the voices of men shouting instructions, I remember feeling no fear—feeling, rather, absolutely safe and protected and surrounded by love.

Where does this memory come from? Was it a tale told so many times in my presence that I simply added myself to the frame?

When I was only a little bit older than that memory, I tried to grow my first flowers from seed. My grandmother, a woman of great gentleness and even temper whether she was soothing a child's skinned knee or wringing the neck of a hen past its laying days for the stewpot, was my inspiration. Or rather the landscape she created was. The front of the house at Ninety Six was always surrounded by flowers—old-fashioned zinnias, black-eyed Susans, bachelor buttons, and more. Slipper trees with their fuzzy burden of flowers. Majestic "snowball" viburnums. (No one ever knew the names of these plants—hence my passion for naming and classification.) This she never called a garden—folk in those days were not so pretentious. It was merely "the yard." The word *garden* she reserved for the expanse out past the hayfield and the stock barns. This space, where she grew the vegetables that she canned for the family, stretched as far as my eyes could see and much farther than my little legs could walk. But when I looked at all that and understood that the source of so much bounty was the tiny little woman with skin the color of pound cake whom I adored, a mighty desire was born in me to be the kind of woman who made things grow.

The plants I grew flowered for a time, then withered and died. The soil of the suburbs seemed little suited to my green dreams. Indeed had I ever articulated a desire to live on the farm as my Mawmaw and Pawpaw and uncle and cousins did, I could've been sure of a good roasting. In the 1960s and '70s, "country" was the worst thing a kid could be—the farm was the place southerners, both African American and white, were leaving as fast as their new city shoes could carry them.

Then suddenly, agonizingly, Pawpaw died—of inoperable colon cancer. Mawmaw had to take up life in the city. And down-home, deep country was lost to me, aside from occasional trips to fish in the pond or check on my uncle's cattle. The house was shut up, almost all the livestock sold, the barns and the smokehouse and all the other outbuildings gradually began falling to ruin.

Over the years I vowed more and more loudly and publicly that someday I'd return—and my mother and father and all my kin scoffed. "Go back to Ninety Six—there's nothing there," they laughed with a single laugh. When I replied the farm was there—"Farming? That's hard work," they scoffed. "You ain't ready for that, little girl."

Ironically the voice of my mother was the loudest of them all. A woman who had grown up chopping cotton, canning the products of her mother's several-acre vegetable plot, and wearing home-sewn fashions, she had learned to despise the dirt that gave her family sustenance—and she'd learned it as much from the strictures that so tightly bound her life as a "colored" girl coming of age in the 1940s as from the picture shows she and her siblings were wild to see every weekend.

Mama, bookish and dreamy as the child she was someday to bear, longed for books and so became first a teacher and then, the pinnacle of her ambition, a librarian. She'd longed for the life of the mind and sacrificed two summers toward a master's degree in library science—before stalling out and sending me, in turn, to the schools where she believed "the best" could be found. Mama had desired glamour and sophistication, and like others of her generation, she found them in wall-to-wall carpeting,

Clarissa Hill Hamilton and Lonnie Hamilton III courted and married at the Hill family farm. Photograph courtesy of the author.

high-heeled shoes, tailored clothing, fur, fine furnishings, and china—all the accoutrements of the successful wife of a respected husband with a snug home in the suburbs of Charleston.

From an early age, it was clear that I, an only child, was to be her crowning achievement, to live her dreams—of travel, of education, of prestige, of everything that she'd felt deprived of. That my journey toward meaning might take me in an arc precisely the *reverse* of hers, back to the red-shouldered hills whose dust she'd been so eager to shake off her clothes, well, that was something I think she found pretty close to unfathomable.

Mama loved the me who traveled abroad. Postcards of *The Blue Boy*, mailed during my residence at the Huntington Library in California. A six-week stay in a villa in Bellagio, surrounded by treasures of the Italian Renaissance. Lightning trips on the train from Charlottesville, Virginia, to New York to take in the theater, the museums. These were the stories to which her heart thrilled. When the talk turned to sustainable agriculture, the farm-to-table movement, my dreams of the marriage of old and new that might make the land in Ninety Six bloom with life once again? Let's just say the conversation faltered.

"You have a P. H. D.," I recall her saying to me in blank incomprehension one day, giving each letter of the title its own separate and emphatic emphasis. "I just can't understand what it is that makes you want to be a *farmer*," speaking the final word with the same measure of horror and disdain she might have given to the word *streetwalker*.

It was only slowly that I came to understand that the mystery of my mother's resistance lay entangled with the life of that dark, desiring woman who had once been enslaved: Eliza. My mother and her sisters avoided all talk, deflected all mention of the researches of their brother and cousins—and finally me—into the facts of Eliza's existence. Those were old times, "slave times," best unmentioned, best forgotten.

By extension the work that women like Eliza did, the work of caring for the land, was seen by Mama's generation, by many generations both before and since, as "slave work"—or in the ugly terms of the time, as "nigger work." Not as labor with dignity and meaning and a system of complex and rich rewards, but as a bondage from which the only escape was flight.

It was a poet and farmer who gave me the words to understand the struggle in which I was engaged, both within my own heart and with those closest to me. Wendell Berry called this prejudice "the hidden wound," the curse that plantation slavery laid upon the hearts of all southerners and upon the land. This wound was what made down-home Ninety Six "the sweetest land there ever was" in the oft-repeated words of cousin Lee Moss: a place where every blade of grass was beloved—but to which it was somehow inconceivable that one's young should ever desire to return.

I take it as a full measure of the love my mother bore for me that, in the month before she died (and that was a year ago last New Year's Day), she forgave me my transgressions—spoke to her brother and sister and instructed them, in spite of all her misgivings, to give me, in language straight out of a southern novel, the bottom land, so that, if farm I must, I'd have the best possible chance of success.

As I was absorbing that final gesture of love, nearly two months to the day after I buried her, I found myself accepting a job offer that would bring me within a twenty-minute drive of the farm my heart has always called home.

My Geechee kin in Charleston would say that it was Mama's spirit that brought me "down home to Ninety Six." I was raised a Geech in Charleston, the Gullah language my first tongue, so I absolutely agree.

When I think of the journey it took to bring me here, I can't help but feel that it lacks much of the drama, the panache, of Cateechee-Issaqueena's ride. But that's actually fine with me. For this time, when the wheel of time turns and the dark, desiring girl comes home, life will not end but begin. Anew. ☽

Sometimes You Just Get Lucky

It was in the deep fall of 1962 when I stepped off the train. The old Columbia terminal is the California Dreaming restaurant now, but then I was twenty-two years old, a Vermont farm boy who'd spent the last several years playing college student at party schools in California, Florida, and Hawaii. Uncle Sam's letter of greetings had arrived a couple of months earlier, delivered as I sunned on the beach at Waikiki. The houseboat I called home was docked nearby in the Ala Wai yacht harbor.

My odyssey was over, and soon I found myself reporting to the Selective Service office back home in the county seat of St. Johnsbury. "You have a talent for news," the army said. "How'd you like to be stationed in New York and work for Public Information at Fort Slocum?"

"I'll take my chances," I told them. "I want to see the world!"

I took my basic training at Fort Dix, New Jersey, and from there was sent to the Armed Forces Information School at Fort Slocum in New York. After graduation I hoped for orders for some exotic location. Columbia, South Carolina, did not come to mind.

Fort Jackson encompasses 5,300 acres of federal land on the northern border of lower Richland. When it was established in 1917, a flagpole was erected in front of the post headquarters, the tallest flagpole in the United States at the time. South Carolina might not have been on my list of places to be stationed, but my three years were good ones. I met and married a beautiful southern girl, Ceille Baird, a USC coed from Moncks Corner. We started a family, and I became editor of the *Fort Jackson Leader*.

Then I made a beeline back to Hawaii to finish school. Only now there'd be no party, no houseboat. The University of Hawaii was tuition-free, but I was a married man now, and families were expensive. I worked several jobs just to make ends meet. One was as a reporter at KHON, the NBC television affiliate in Honolulu.

One night I woke Ceille to ask if she were homesick. "Me too," I told her. "Let's go home."

"Where's home?" she asked. And without hesitation I answered, "South Carolina."

A Realtor friend located a heavily forested plot of land in Lower Richland at the crest of a Vermont-like hill. "You're going to love it," she said, and how very right she was.

Sometimes you just get lucky.

From Columbia we drove past the VA hospital, past rolling fields and farms. There was the Burnside Farm, McGregor's Dairy Farm, and, on both sides of the divided highway, miles of hay fields, pastures, and pecan groves. There were beef cattle farms with Black Angus and white-faced Herefords and several large horse farms with glistening, white-fenced paddocks of well-groomed horses.

We drove past McEntire Air National Guard Base, which covers a large part of Beulah Plantation, one of the early plantations of Lower Richland. A few miles farther we turned left, off the highway and into the sandhills region. The land connects to Tom's Creek, which for the most part flows north to south. It proved to be a treasure trove of deciduous and mixed forest, wild critters, and history. There were loblolly and longleaf pines, ancient white oaks, hickories, gum trees and bays, cedars and hollies. In a stream two otters played slip and slide. There were deer and wild turkeys and coveys of bobwhite quail. We built our home on land that had been part of "The Sandhills," a three-thousand-acre plantation belonging to Keziah Goodwyn Hopkins Brevard, once the wealthiest woman in Richland County. Her story was documented in *A Plantation Mistress on the Eve of the Civil War*.

A father-son hike in the late 1970s delivered more recent history. Walking our dogs deep in the valley, James, a teen at the time, came to a stop.

"What's this?" he wanted to know.

"Well," I said, "there's a barrel, and there's some copper tubing and over here by the spring are some mason jars and old buckets. Son, I'd say you have just discovered a moonshine still. And it was not too long ago the lawmen found it and put their axes to it, from the looks of the slashed barrels."

The whole of Lower Richland consists of 350 square miles of hills, valleys, fields, forests, and floodplain. There's Fort Jackson on the north,

The author's son, James, at an abandoned moonshine still. Photograph courtesy of Jim Welch.

the Congaree River on the south, the Columbia city limits on the west, and the Wateree River on the east. This was plantation country in the seventeenth and eighteenth centuries, and a few were spared by Sherman's forces.

The Congaree National Park, one of our country's newest national parks, boasts some of the tallest trees in the east. It's the largest tract of old-growth bottomland hardwood forest in the United States. While filming a segment of the public television series *NatureScene,* naturalist Rudy Mancke and I entered the base of an overcup oak and were able to stand upright. We discussed the tree from inside it!

There in the swamp, the elevation above sea level is only 130 feet, but a few miles northeast is Cook's Mountain at 374 feet. John Lawson, the English explorer, observed it in 1700. "We came to the most amazing prospect I had seen in Carolina," he wrote. "One alp with a top like a sugar loaf advanced its head above all the rest considerably."

During a Cook's Mountain nature walk in the mid-1990s, I watched famed botanist Wade Batson pick the leaves from a vine of poison ivy.

"I never was allergic to this," he said. A few minutes later he handed me a clump of sour grass to taste, which I did, suddenly remembering he'd picked the poison ivy with the same hand. "I don't think I'm allergic, either," I said, trying to call up memories of a lifetime of summers. Apparently I am one of the 15 percent who are not. Sometimes you do get lucky.

Summer is a deep green here. It's everywhere you look. It's down the hill and across the valley. It grows up through fallen dogwood blossoms and over any remnants of flowering spring. We've lived on this place forty-two years now. From here we've watched the seasons come and go. Fall with its splashes of muted colors, orange and yellow and gold. Winter with its denuded limbs, their outlines stark across the white sky, on occasion covered with a heavy blanket of snow.

It's here I finally saw the elusive fox squirrel, the largest of the North American tree squirrels, with its black head, white nose, and big, bushy tail. I'd waited such a long time to observe one in my woods, and suddenly there he was gathering hickory nuts at the edge of my lawn.

It's here I witnessed coveys of quail exploding from the underbrush; here I watched herds of deer devouring my lantana, and here I entertained friends with croquet and tea while a six-foot-long coachwhip snake crawled out from under the deck. Here I heard Hurricane Hugo popping the trees in half at midnight, and the next day, surveying the damage, saw a frightened bobcat run out from under a fallen oak.

Here we've loved our children and our grandchildren and now our great-grandchildren. Here where summer is a deep green. ☽

Jane F. Zenger

My Wild Life in Cedar Creek

I live on the edge of a magical forest about twenty miles from Columbia, South Carolina. In mid-April the forest comes alive. The deciduous trees suddenly unfurl fresh leaves that shade the undergrowth, and mushrooms pop up. The ferns unfurl, and the river bamboo spikes up on the sandy shores of the creek. Fireflies light the evenings in sync, and butterflies emerge from cocoons looking for early blossoms. Tiny ring-necked snakes warm themselves on flat rocks; speckled fawns hide behind their wary mothers. If you live in such a place, you might want to pay attention.

Many years ago I started an annual ritual, and every Easter morning I take a walk to observe the unveiling of springtime. With my journal and camera, I explore the twelve acres my husband, Steve, and I bought from friends in 1988, on the edge of Cedar Creek. It is mainly the wildflowers I want to see, for they are open for business only a few days, and then they are gone for another year.

We knew this property from our college days, having fallen in love with it when three friends purchased the original eighty-acre tract. We were all students or faculty members at USC then. During those years we hiked the property and enjoyed peaceful parties at their hundred-year-old farmhouse. We danced to bluegrass music and feasted on vegetarian dinners and Frogmore stew. Steve and I never imagined we could find such beautiful land on a deep creek surrounded by mature hardwoods and abundant wildlife. So when our friends called us in Texas, where we were working, to say they were willing to part with twelve acres of their pristine property, we didn't think twice. If we had been living in Austin, it might have been a hard sell, but Houston, with the traffic and crime, was easy to put in the rearview mirror. This was our chance to move home to South Carolina and

Cedar Creek atamasco lilies, April 2016. Photograph by Larry Cameron.

live close enough to commute to Columbia for work but in a rural setting with neighbors we loved.

Cedar Creek has established families and newcomers drawn by its natural beauty. The community itself is old. The first settlers came from Charleston and other lowcountry towns in the 1700s, I've been told, with grants from King George III. They claimed large tracts and started farms, clearing the hardwood forests and planting crops that eventually depleted the soil. I pass two historic churches every day: Cedar Creek United Methodist, built in 1761, and Oak Grove Methodist, 1891. Many descendants of the founding families still attend and care for the church buildings and cemeteries. There are Revolutionary War stories and Civil War tales about brave women and children saving their schools and homes from Sherman's fires. Most of the rural roads are named for the old farming and business families—Graddick, Lever, Muller, Dubard, Loner, Frick.

I appreciate Cedar Creek's history, but I know there were migrations of indigenous people long before those European families arrived. They fished, hunted, and followed the game along the tributaries of the three rivers coming together in the midlands. They probably hunted along the banks of these ancient watershed areas now known as Horse Creek, Little Cedar Creek, and Big Cedar Creek and the nameless smaller streams that eventually join and flow into the Broad River. It's not unusual after a rain or digging in the garden to find white flakes or worked quartz points. While digging the foundation for our house, Steve unearthed two four-inch spear points—rhyolite, most likely from the Savannah River period. One of the most beautiful points we found is a Kirk-stemmed pure white quartz point, sharp enough to cut leather. Artifact expert Jim Maus helped me identify what we've found. It is overwhelming to think I am holding a tool created between 8000 and 10000 B.C. Another favorite, a slender, milky quartz Guilford point, is relatively new—left by hunters only about 3000–6000 B.C. One can't help but wonder how these early residents lived, loved, and survived primitive conditions—and a land of black bears, cougars, and wolves. All that's left of the big predators now, it seems, are the land developers pushing their gated communities and golf courses out of Blythewood in this direction.

After all these years, I still don't know many people outside our secluded neighborhood. Because we don't farm or do much business in Blythewood, we don't really know many of the prominent families. In my commute I pass long driveways and private dirt roads that wind back to some old farmhouse or family community like ours. When people come to visit us for the first time, they are cocky about using their GPSes, but those will only get them so far. When the gravel county road runs out, there are still tricky divided lanes and a long dirt drive that curves through cedars, dogwoods, and holly trees before you come to our back door. Once you might have been greeted by several dogs, three to five cats, a small flock of chickens, an overly friendly duck, and an emu. Now with the children gone, we have scaled back to a few lazy cats.

Cedar Creek's temperature is usually ten degrees colder than surrounding regions. That means plants and animals thrive here that actually belong in a swamp, the Appalachians, or on the sandy coastal plain. None of my naturalist friends could ever give me a good explanation about the climate variation. They mention a "dip" or that the land rises 321 feet above sea level. Whatever the reason, the temperature is usually cooler than anywhere nearby. When Joe Pinner was the regular weatherman on WIS-TV, he often mentioned that although it might be forty degrees in Columbia, it would be a frosty thirty degrees in Cedar Creek. Whenever someone learned I lived in Cedar Creek, they inevitably asked about our weather.

During one pounding hailstorm, I called the NBC/WIS weather line and got the man himself on the phone. "Joe," I said. "I'm out here in Cedar Creek and the hail is pelting my house and shredding my vegetable

Cedar Creek close-up. Photograph by Larry Cameron.

garden." He asked about the size of the pellets. I stepped out on the porch and picked up a piece that had ricocheted close to the door. "It looks like the size of a peanut M&M," I replied. Five minutes later Joe delivered his report, saying he'd just heard from Jane Zenger in Cedar Creek that peanut M&Ms were falling on her house. I was teased for months.

Joe, who lives nearby, is fond of Cedar Creek. He says it's where the people have the coldest feet and warmest hearts in South Carolina.

Our property lies where the coastal plain, sandhills, and piedmont touch. Cedar Creek is the western boundary, and the deep ravine adds to the region's diversity. Steve and I designed our house during the year it took to sell our tract house in Houston and for me to find a teaching position in Columbia. His gift from me was a year clearing the property and building a passive solar house with natural cypress siding, large windows, and sixteen-foot ceilings. Our house sits on a tabletop ridge seventy-five feet above Big Cedar Creek, a primary perennial stream that drains Little

Cedar and Horse Creeks. I can walk out the back door and within a minute enter a hardwood forest where early Native Americans might have lived and hunted thousands of years ago. At the woods' edge, a downhill path leads to the water. The hike is steep, and as you get closer to the bank, you need to grab saplings to avoid falling over the edge. Once at the edge, you can find your footing on a narrow path forged by deer, dogs, and other animals. Then you can walk at least a mile in either direction without running into civilization. Across the creek is a pasture where the Bloom family occasionally keeps cows and coyotes train their young pups to hunt.

When our children were growing up, they found a narrow otter slide where they could shimmy over the edge and catch enough roots to climb down to the water. Then they could jump rock to rock, build dams, and swing across to the other side on the rope we tied on an overhanging limb. In the summer when the water was low, the neighbors joined us for creek walking adventures, donning old tennis shoes to explore up- and downstream. The sandbars were the best places to find rocks, bones, and freshwater clams. After high water floods, we'd find interesting items in low-hanging branches. We used my father's old Boy Scout reference book with illustrations of animal prints to key out anything that wasn't obvious. Evidence of raccoon, opossum, bird, deer, and dog (or coyote) prints gave us an idea of what went on down there when we were busy up on the hill.

The southwest side of the property is different altogether. Another path leads to one of three ephemeral intermediate feeder streams that eventually spill into the big creek. There is less sun and therefore little undergrowth. The beech, cedar, and giant American holly trees in this valley are getting old, and limbs and fallen trees litter the forest floor. Here, where the mint green luna moths propagate, is where I find the best wild violets and trout lilies.

During the early 1990s, a sustained drought started affecting the pines and dogwoods. The pines became more susceptible to the pine beetle, and one spring many older dogwoods didn't leaf out. The impending beetle infestation meant we had to timber several acres of pines. I don't like cutting trees, but I knew just the professional to call. Jeff Brown, a forester who lived here when his children were growing up, was the only logger I trusted to take the infected trees. I knew he would leave the maple, dogwood, holly, and old cedar stands unblemished. He explained that although this area was clear-cut for farming more than a hundred years ago, the steep creekside slopes protected many of the old hardwoods on hillsides where farming wouldn't be feasible. That's why much of our forest

All trees have purpose and repurpose in Cedar Creek. Photograph by Larry Cameron.

could replenish itself and many of the old trees survived. Jeff also could explain why my expensive apple trees did not produce: cedar apple rust disease. Of course the pears I planted have thrived—with fruit so hard and grainy I usually leave them for the deer.

We have scores of dead trees standing. They're bare and hollow, full of holes that make perfect nurseries for barred owls, squirrels, and raccoons. Every few years we watch baby animals pop in and out of them. That's why we let those old trees stand until they fall on their own, unless they're near the road or close to the garden shed or chicken house.

A geographical crossroad, Cedar Creek has sand, clay, and chunks of white quartz but very little topsoil for gardening. Granite outcrops twenty feet tall form rock canyons overlooking the creek bed. Three ecosystems are visible within a two-minute walk into the woods. On one mixed-up hilltop, I can stand within an arm's reach of swamp azalea, coastal yucca, and mountain laurel making nice with each other. If the spring transition is warm and moist, the mountain laurel explodes. We expect to be inundated by pink blossoms.

Dr. Gail Wagner is an ethnobotanist at the University of South Carolina. She is also a dear friend who lived more than a decade in a log cabin within a ten-minute walk of my house. Exploring the woods with Gail was humbling. I know a little about the plants and wildflowers, but Gail sees everything in three dimensions. She knows the plants, when they bloom, and if they were used for food or medicine by the early settlers or Native Americans.

"Cedar Creek vegetation is unexpected and entirely fascinating to a botanist," Gail wrote when I asked her what she loved about this place. "Reminiscent of a cove forest in the southern Appalachians, it includes species not normally found in the Piedmont of central South Carolina. The herb understory is especially rich: I love the fairy-fantastic spring displays of flowers coupled with the earlier appearance of clumps of salamander eggs in vernal puddle-ponds." Gail reeled off the names of her favorite Cedar Creek plants: adder's-tongue, jack-in-the-pulpit, pawpaw, trout lily, southern sugar maple, wild iris, mayapple, bloodroot, bellwort, sweet shrub, wild ginger, mountain laurel, lousewort, and others. "I'd say the biggest surprise to me was when Steve came up to me with *Stewartia* (wild camellia) in his buttonhole, and an even bigger surprise was to discover that large patches can be found in the area."

On this year's Easter walk, I found blooming trout lilies, atamasco lilies, bluets, pink oxalis (wood sorrel), buckeyes, wild violets, rue anemone, sweet shrub, and columbine. I have a little chicken-wire cage around the rare pink Catesby trillium that has bloomed every year since I discovered it fifteen years ago.

Through the years we have experienced some unusual animal visitations. Lee Lou arrived one cold foggy morning. The ground and creek had been frozen solid for days, and we were taking our time getting out of bed. Our son, Jay, must have been about twelve or thirteen, and he started calling us urgently from the kitchen window. "Mom! Dad! There is a dinosaur in the yard." We're a family of practical jokers, so we assumed this was a ploy to get us up to make breakfast. But then he yelled, "No, it's not a dinosaur, it must be an ostrich." We sat up and started looking for our boots. Then we heard him say confidently, "Nope, not an ostrich, it is definitely an emu." By then we were on the way down the steps. Sure enough, outside the kitchen window we saw an emu, kicking at a frozen puddle, apparently looking for water.

The Cedar Creek children pose for their annual Christmas photo, 2007. Photograph courtesy of the author.

By then Jay's sister, Katie, was up. We looked at each other. The emu must be hungry and thirsty. We wanted to catch it. Steve was not convinced. He looked at me and the excited children. "No way," he said. "Don't even think about it. I am having nothing to do with this," and he disappeared back upstairs. Two hours later Katie, Jay, and I had used corn and buckets of water to lure the two-hundred-pound bird into the winter garden. Lee Lou lived with us for almost a year before a local rancher 'fessed up and claimed her.

When the seasons change, or before a storm, our property becomes a natural freeway for migrating animals. Turtles the size of army helmets pass through with wild turkeys, opossum, fox, raccoon families, and herds of deer. Golden coyotes lope along the edge of the yard looking me in the eye, seemingly unconcerned that I am watching them from my back porch. Any snake that is common to this area has shown up at some point.

Then there are the birds. Almost every evening we hear barred owls keeping track of each other. The pileated woodpeckers pounding away are noisy enough, but their prehistoric-sounding night calls will scare the jeepers out of you. Red-tailed hawks circle overhead, looking for baby rabbits or field mice. Phoebes build nests under the eaves, and scores of small songbirds visit the feeders. Bluebirds and scarlet tanagers seem to be declining, but a mob of annoying crows moved in recently. They are obnoxious bullies but harmless. Last year I took a late afternoon walk down an abandoned road into an area I hadn't explored in years. The woods were quiet and dark. I rounded a corner and felt an eerie sensation. I looked up into an old loblolly pine. There must have been fifty or more buzzards looking down at me, silent as a graveyard.

There are six homes at the end of the dirt road where we have lived for almost thirty years. We are close friends with our neighbors and the six children who grew up together like a tribe of extended brothers and sisters. Looking back, I realize how they were influenced by our cast of characters. They didn't need the Internet. If they wanted to know anything, they'd ask a neighbor. They thought it was natural to have walking encyclopedias next door. Within five minutes they could find an archeologist, geologist, wildlife writer, nature photographer, forester, librarian, ethnobotanist, two teachers, and, in case someone needed legal advice, an attorney.

All six of those children have stayed close, even though they're adults now and out on their own. The families gather for holidays, and visits include walks in the woods to see a favorite tree or "reading rock." Far from shops and sidewalks, they learned other lessons.

"Growing up in the middle of the woods just made nature make sense to me," one of those grown children, Hannah Cameron, told me. "It isn't always predictable, and you can't always trust it—but I learned very early that was okay. The bugs were supposed to be everywhere, the creeks were supposed to flood sometimes, and some days you legitimately couldn't get to school because a huge tree fell over your one-lane gravel driveway and the neighborhood men had to all show up with their chainsaws and tractors to haul it away. But that's how life is sometimes too. Some days were perfect in the middle of nowhere, some days weren't, but we learned to find the joy behind the simplicity, and if we couldn't find it, we had to find a way to create it on our own."

Cedar Creek has taught them well. ꙍ

Picnic on the Sandbar, giclée on canvas, © 2001 by John Carroll Doyle. Courtesy of the John Carroll Doyle Art Gallery.

Island People

"This is better, home here. Me and my wife been together all these years now, sixty years. Long water run out me eye how thankful the Lord been to me! I sleep so good here, the world turn over."

Bubberson Brown, dates unknown, from *And I'm Glad: An Oral History of Edisto Island,* by Nick Lindsay

CJ Lyons

An Enchantment of Light

"New skies the exile finds, but the heart remains the same."

Horace, *Epistles,* book 1, no. 11

There are three bridges to reach my home in Coligny. The first two take me from the mainland to Hilton Head Island. Often crowded with visitors (which technically, after almost nine years here, I guess I still qualify as), it can be easy to miss the ever-changing spectacle nature provides. But the final bridge, a high-arched span from Spanish Wells along Palmetto Bay, takes my breath away every single time.

I'll never forget the first time I crossed it at night. I was coming home from dinner with friends in Moss Creek, and the highway was empty. I sped up the bridge at an angle that pointed my car directly at the sickle moon that had gathered the stars into its crescent embrace. I thought if I could only gain enough speed, I'd shoot straight into the heavens. It was a magical moment—the first of many here in my new home in the low-country. I felt as if my little Subaru had wings.

Back when I was a flight doctor, I loved flying at night. In fact the first time I almost died was on a night like that one on the bridge. Clear skies, a blanket of stars.

☽ ☽ ☽

All my life I've suffered from a restless soul, leaving my rural Pennsylvania home and family behind when I was only seventeen. They have lived for generations nestled in the small towns of the Allegheny Mountains, scattered between Altoona and Pittsburgh along back roads with colorful names like Rattlesnake Pike and Devil's Elbow. I felt like a traitor leaving them to go to college, but my heart was torn between my need to see more of the world and my love for a family with roots sunk deeper than any coal mine.

A storyteller all my life, my inability to discriminate between fact and fiction led to quite a number of time-outs and parent-teacher conferences when I was a child. Telling stories, listening to those voices in my head, was my way, as an extreme introvert, of understanding and coping with the chaos surrounding me. I wrote my first novel in high school and two more science fiction novels in medical school, none of which have ever seen the light of day, thankfully.

I never dreamed I'd turn my quirky hobby into a second career. It was a magnificent dream come true to have made it through college and med school and become a pediatrician—surely that was enough to ask from life. I even toyed with the idea of giving up writing, but like any addict, I couldn't. As soon as I tried, new characters and ideas would hammer at my mind until I brought them to life, even if I was the only one who was reading my stories.

Then, during my pediatric internship back home in Pittsburgh, everything changed. Writing became more than a strange sideline that was difficult to explain or talk about; it became my lifeline, pulling me from a morass of grief and pain back onto the shores of sanity.

The life of an intern is nothing like what you see on TV. We live separate from the rest of the world, working at night while normal people sleep, making life-and-death decisions about little babies, choices that will affect their families forever. We speak a different language; we become our own family. Halfway through my internship year, we lost one of our family. Murdered. A crime so vicious it made headlines across the nation.

After Jeff's death, we all struggled to find balance in a suddenly out-of-kilter world where nothing was safe to take for granted. As always I turned to my writing to guide me out of the black abyss of grief, but science fiction no longer held the magic it once had. I needed to understand evil and bloodlust and injustice. I needed heroes who were ordinary people finding the courage to stand up and make a difference. Inspired by my patients and their families, all real-life heroes, I wrote my first novel, a thriller titled *Borrowed Time,* and found my new path.

It was a path that eventually led me to a land of enchantment, a thousand miles from home, here in South Carolina's lowcountry.

ꙮ ꙮ ꙮ

It was a New Year's Eve, the first time I almost died. It wouldn't be the last—by the time I left medicine, after seventeen years as a pediatric ER doc and community pediatrician, I'd faced many dangers caused by both nature and humans.

This night was crisp and cold, the kind of cold that made the stars shimmer as we flew in our STATAngel helicopter out to pick up a newborn.

"This baby sounds pretty sick, doc," Zane, our pilot, said over the radio. "Want me to make up a song for it?"

Despite the fact that Zane couldn't carry a tune to save his life, it was an offer we never refused. We believed in the power of his crazy, improvised songs, just as we each had our own good luck charms and magical rituals and believed in the power of jet fuel to get us back home to Children's Hospital safe and sound. When we were in our helicopter, racing the stars, high above the mere mortals below, we believed we could handle anything.

♪ ♪ ♪

It was seven moves and five cities later before I found the courage to aim for publication. But thanks to friends who were bestselling authors, I soon found myself with two contracts from a major New York publisher and a choice to make: after seventeen years of practicing medicine, should I take a chance and build a new career as an author, or focus on my patients and give up writing? A painful choice to make, but I knew I could not continue to give both my patients and my writing 120 percent of my energy and focus.

I took the leap of faith and left medicine to pursue that second dream come true. Of course the first thing to decide was where I would live. As a writer I knew it would be difficult to get a mortgage since the income stream is so unpredictable (read: fickle). It was time for this restless soul to find a permanent home.

Where else would I choose but the one place that had captivated me since I first visited for a medical conference? The wide beaches of Hilton Head Island.

I've spent most of my life in the mountains of the Rust Belt, but as soon as I visited Hilton Head, I felt like I was home. More than the beach or the gentle waves or the gorgeous foliage, it was the light that enchanted me. From the delicate apricot mist announcing the sunrise to the midday vibrancy transforming the water to brilliant cerulean to the crisp violet sunset shadows, the light was intoxicating, and I could not drink my fill of it.

Sunrise on Hilton Head Island. Photograph by Toni McGee Causey.

◡ ◡ ◡

Before you fly for the first time, there are rituals you must attend to. The flight nurses in charge of our orientation laughingly called these our "burial rites."

First they fit you for a Nomex flight suit. It's a clingy fabric totally foreign to Mother Nature. Hot in the summer, cold in the winter, once you wear it for the first time you'll never be able to wash it clean of the stench of adrenalin and fear-soaked sweat. No one looks good in Nomex, but you don't wear it for fashion. You wear it so that if the helicopter you're riding in catches fire, you might gain a few seconds to make it out alive.

Next comes the paperwork. Next of kin. Distinguishing scars they might identify you by since the Nomex doesn't protect your face. Name and address of your dentist. Just in case, they say. We're sure we'll never need it. But just in case.

☽ ☽ ☽

May 5, 2006. My independence day. I moved a thousand miles from friends and family to my new home, an inexpensive fixer-upper condo in the Coligny area of Hilton Head. Despite entering a land that appeared draped in a magical cloak of color and light, not everything was rosy with my new career as a full-time writer. My dream debut, a hardcover novel that seemed to have everything going for it, from a dozen stunning cover quotes from *New York Times* bestselling authors to excellent preorders from all the major bookstores, was unceremoniously pulled from publication about ninety days before its launch. Why? Something totally out of my control: cover art issues.

So here I was, a thousand miles away from anyone I knew (other than my Realtor), suddenly unemployed for the first time since I was fifteen. What could I do?

I did what I always did. I wrote. But now I had a new ally—my new home.

As I rehabilitated (in every sense of the word) my condo, which initially resembled a crime scene more than a residence, I also took long walks, exploring. The beach here is so alive; it's a different beach each time you walk it. Such a variety of creatures to watch—and I'm not talking about the tourists who visit in the summer. I'll never forget the Christmas a few years after moving when I woke to hundreds, maybe thousands, of jewel-toned jellyfish scattered like ornaments across the white sand as if angels had decided to decorate for the holiday.

Those first few months, the beach saved my sanity. I painted one wall of my living room with a metallic paint in the exact blue as the tidal pools reflecting the midday sky. Every time I sat down to write, that wall made me smile. I brought magnolia buds and cuttings of wild confederate jasmine into my home, their perfume intoxicating. I watched the sweetgrass turn purple in the fall and the way the Spartina grass changed color with the moods of the sun and tide. I learned new names: loblolly pine, live oak (my new favorite tree), camellia (flowers in December? who knew!), oleander, crape myrtle.

Each day I walked among beauty, my imagination soaring with the birds that also were new to me: cormorants, herons, sandpipers, ospreys, cranes, gulls, and, of course, the always comical pelicans. And each day, inspired by my surroundings and refusing to give up on my dream, I wrote.

☽ ☽ ☽

Helicopters have no wings. Obvious, of course, but you don't really think about it until the machine you're depending on to keep you airborne begins to act like a recalcitrant toddler throwing a tantrum. We'd reached the small-town hospital, made good time thanks to Zane's expert piloting, and were approaching the LZ—the landing zone local police and hospital security guards had set up in the parking lot beside their ER.

"Help me out," Zane said. "Watch for lines." When we landed in a makeshift LZ, power lines hidden from above were our greatest fear. It was every crewmember's duty to let the pilot know if any lurked nearby.

I was on the side closest to the hospital walls, which would be the most likely place for outside power lines to come into the building. I pressed my face against the Lexan window and scanned the inky black night surrounding us as we descended. Down, down, all good, no lines, no visible danger. We touched the ground, and I let out the breath I'd been holding.

And then we went spinning, out of control.

Turns out the greatest danger wasn't in the air but in the black ice the locals had neglected to clear from our landing site—a site precariously close to the building. If our tail rotor hit it . . . images of every helicopter crash from every movie swarmed over me. *Watch the rotor, never walk toward the rotor, that tail rotor is what will get you killed*—warnings the pilots hammered into us civilians.

Before I could blink, we shot back up into the air, the brick wall of the hospital skimming my vision, so close, too close. And then, thanks to Zane's quick reflexes, we were clear. Stars and the moon embraced us as we hovered above our brush with death.

A few minutes later we landed properly, whisked the baby away, and took off once more. "Angel Four en route to Children's," Zane informed traffic control. "Five souls on board, all safe and sound."

☽ ☽ ☽

If there was one thing I learned from Jeff's death, it was that life goes on. After my first book was canceled, I wallowed in self-pity for a few days and kept writing. It was hard going for a while, but how could I possibly think of leaving my new home? Every time I had to go off-island, even for the short trip to Bluffton (the guys at Lowe's knew me by name by the time I finished renovations), I'd feel a shockwave of angst as I drove over the bridge to the mainland. The Spartina grass shining green and gold intertwined with the brown of the tidal mudflats and the soft blue water seemed to be waving me back, warning me against leaving Brigadoon.

I'd finish my errands and return home, feeling a sense of belonging, often murmuring out loud (not too loudly for fear of tempting fate), "I live in paradise!"

Oh, and just to let you know that karma has a sense of humor, that first book I wrote while living here after I'd lost my dream debut? It hit number two on the *New York Times* bestseller list, stayed there for seven weeks, sold a quarter of a million copies, and won several major awards. Since then I've gone on to publish more than forty of my "Thrillers with Heart," including that canceled book (albeit three years after it was originally scheduled to be released). My books have touched millions of people—far more than I could impact treating one patient at a time.

As I pace the beach, dreaming up new murder and mayhem for my fictional alter egos, the sights, sounds, and smells of this island have woven themselves into my own character. Just as I can never imagine giving up writing, I never want to leave my island of enchantment.

Proof that there is a cure for wanderlust: if you define home as where your family lives, then the mountains of Pennsylvania will always be my home. If you define home as where your heart lives and where your soul flourishes, then I've found a second home walking the beaches of Hilton Head Island. This restless soul is content to remain here, under these cerulean blue skies. ➴

Sallie Ann Robinson

Sweet Home Daufuskie

Say what you want about places, but my go-to favorite in South Carolina is one I call home. Daufuskie Island is one of several small barrier islands off the Atlantic coast. To this day there is no bridge that connects it to the mainland. You have to get to and from there by boat.

Life on Daufuskie is sweet. There's no traffic to deal with or sirens all times of the day and night. There are no shopping centers or grocery stores on every corner. It's a place to kick back, take your shoes off, and relax. Folks love to visit, and some make it their home—getting away from the hustle and bustle of city life.

The island is rich with a history that goes back to the Indians who dominated it in the 1600s and 1700s. For many generations Gullah folks lived and farmed on Daufuskie, surviving the best way they knew.

Big, old oak trees draped in beautiful Spanish moss shade the winding dirt roads. The beach is beautiful too. It has a long stretch of soft white sand and a pleasant breeze that blows in from the Atlantic Ocean. Depending on which side of the island you're on, you can look to the left of Calibogue Sound and see the famous Hilton Head Island or right and see Tybee Island. On the south side of the island, beyond the marsh and creeks, you can see Savannah.

When you look across the sounds, both Hilton Head and Savannah seem to be within arm's reach. But it takes a boat ride of twenty to thirty minutes to get to and from. Maybe that's why Daufuskie has been a secret getaway for so many years.

The island has no streetlights. On a dark night, you cannot see your hands in front of your face. On nights when the moon is full, the air feels mellow, and the moonlight gives you a magical feeling. Pop used to say

132

One of Daufuskie's famous dirt roads. Photograph courtesy of the author.

Daufuskie is so quiet that sometimes you can almost hear when a rat is peeing on cotton.

The island's rich soil no longer gets plowed and farmed like it did when I was growing up. That was in the late 1950s and '60s. Farmers back then planted big fields of corn, collards, okra, tomatoes, sweet potatoes, peanuts, and much more. All our vegetables were organic. Mungen Creek and the Cooper River still supply great seafood—shrimps, fish, crabs, oysters, and conch. But the people now don't rely on wild game like we did. We had raccoon and squirrel for dinner.

I am sixth-generation born and raised on Daufuskie, and growing up there gave me so much to be thankful for today. We lived off the land, the woods, and the ocean and worked hard to survive. Even though we had very little, we were never without. Folks valued all they had and did not mind sharing when needed.

Most of the day was spent getting things done, not talking yourself out of doing what was important. Parents and neighbors taught us how not to take anything for granted. We were given tough love and fresh food. Everyone looked out for one another in good or bad times.

The author on her island. Photograph courtesy of Sallie Ann Robinson.

Kids did as they were told and acted accordingly. Adults made all the decisions, and children abided by their rules at all times. Our elders shared their stories and taught us to be leaders and kind to others. Manners and respect were not just preached but practiced, because it was about pride and proof of being raised right in the home.

Folks did not have degrees to prove they were good at what they did. They had their pride for their work and the people they served. The woods were our playground, and we treasured all they had to offer. Besides the vegetables we grew, the island supplied us with wild berries, plums, grapes, and nuts that were plentiful in season. We went to church most Sundays to worship and to be thankful—and we couldn't wait to get home to sit down at the table for a big dinner.

My last year on Daufuskie, I was taught by a great teacher named Pat Conroy. It was my best year of school. He taught and showed us things way beyond the world we lived in and how things were going to be very different once we left. Today I treasure all he taught me, because he was right. The world was very different off the island. It was much busier in

Savannah and Bluffton, where I lived while finishing middle and high school. And it was busier yet in Philadelphia, where I lived for three years and went to more school, for fashion design and nursing.

When I left Daufuskie in 1970, I learned a very important thing about myself. I learned I was Gullah. That word wasn't part of our teaching or our vocabulary. I also learned I was part Indian, so my heritage connected me to the very folks I grew up with. I have an everlasting respect for those folks, and even though it was hard being in Savannah that first year, I realized Daufuskie children could do things city kids couldn't. For instance, I could drive a cow. That's how I learned to drive a car. We had wagons, and we had to learn to keep the cows straight in the roads. I laugh when I think about it.

These days I make my home in Savannah. I chose Savannah because it isn't far from home, and I've got easy access to an airport. But I miss home every day. I miss the feeling of walking down one of the long, quiet, winding dirt roads and taking a shortcut to places we used to play. I miss the peace, the non-crime, the closeness you have with folks you know and can trust. It was the love that made everybody feel equal.

I know progress brings changes, and sometimes changes are needed, but most of the time they're not needed as much as some people think. I pray Daufuskie does not overgrow. I pray it will stay in the beautiful state it has always been in. I think the people I knew on Daufuskie would pray the same way, too. ☽

☾

A Lesson from Ole Jones

Nestled beneath towering live oaks interspersed with tall palmettos is my second home on Seabrook Island. It has a commanding view of the Bohicket River, the old village of Rockville, and the North Edisto Inlet. Our home is located on a forty-acre tract with only one other home, the oldest on the island, owned by my friend Larry Bradham. It took me two years to buy the lot from him, which was six hundred feet from his home.

When I showed him my house plans—a simple two-story lowcountry affair—he shrugged and said okay. Then he told me the story of my just-purchased lot. It had been the Seabrook wharf, and the overseer lived in a house on it. Sea island cotton, indigo, and vegetables were shipped from the old wharf.

In 1897 the overseer's wife became infuriated at something and started a fire that burned the house down. The island owner built a new house for the overseer. It was finished in 1898 and is now lived in by Bradham and his vivacious wife, Cassandra.

So the lot sat there for more than a hundred years before I bought it in 2000. When I finished the house, we had the Bradhams over for drinks, and he brought me a picture of the original house that burned. My new house and the old one were almost identical! I looked at my wife, Pat, and said, "Hope you don't start playing with matches!"

The setting is second heaven. Seabrook is a lovely island next to Kiawah Island, its famous and posh neighbor. Not as tourist-oriented as Kiawah, Seabrook still has great golf courses, an equestrian center, and for me, an avid cyclist, miles of great roads.

To me it is a combination of setting and people that make a place.

Seabrook's small full-time population is a diverse mix of retirees primarily from New Jersey and the mid-Atlantic states and locals, which means you were raised nearby. Locals include fishermen, shrimpers, retailers, and tradesmen. This blending of northerners and locals makes for some interesting interactions. At times you think the Civil War is still active.

The cross-section of people on these islands is immense. Here are native blacks with Gullah-laced accents, New Jerseyites with the patois of Uzis, New Yorkers who generally think all southerners are inbred because of our slow drawls, shrill-tongued midwesterners, and foreigners who are aloof to it all, planted among us Carolina and Georgia folk and proper Charlestonians.

Sometimes I will put my bike in the boat and cross the Bohicket to ride on Wadmalaw Island, where Rockville is. About five minutes by boat from Seabrook, Wadmalaw is a large sea island sparsely populated because of heavy restrictions on building. It has a large African American population, many quite poor.

Two Wadmalaw islanders regularly fish at my dock from their rough metal boat. Moses is seventy-six; Gabriel eighty. They always ask my permission to fish there, and I always tell them, "Fellows, you are in the water and you own that so you never have to ask me."

One fine summer morning, I went out to my fishing boat. It's thirty feet, with a pair of massive 250-horsepower Mercury engines. Moses and Gabriel were there. I thought for a moment. "Guys," I said, "I am going out to the reef. Would you like to go with me?"

They were aghast. The reef is about a mile out from the sea buoy. Gabriel was a little reluctant, his face showing white stubble. "I never been in the ocean!" Now, here is a man who has lived on Wadmalaw (they call it "de Wadmaalaaw") for his eighty years. But I knew there were old people there who had never been off the island even though it is only thirty minutes from Charleston.

"We will be perfectly safe. This boat is big." I demonstrated the radio where I could call the Coast Guard. "You fellows need nothing. I have all the rods and reels you need."

Gabriel said he would prefer his own stuff, and they finally climbed aboard the boat. I could tell Gabriel was nervous. Not Moses, who has spent a great deal of his life working on shrimp boats.

Fishing is sometimes iffy, but when we dropped our lines at the reef, it was on. For the next three hours, we caught three dozen rock bass, trout, and red drum. One drum weighed twenty-five pounds, and we released it.

Ginny's Fresh Air Market. Oil on canvas by Bob LeFevre. Courtesy of the artist.

When we got back, I knew I had been blessed. Gabriel and Moses expertly cleaned and filleted the fish on my dock. I let them have ninety percent of the catch.

The next day I saw a note pinned to my cleaning station. "Mr. Wheeler we had a wonderful time. If you look in your boat you will see we repaired your cast net. Thank you and may the Lord bless you and your family." Signed in wobbling handwriting, "Moses."

I discovered the Charleston area in the 1950s during one of my breaks from the University of South Carolina. And while I liked Charleston, what drew me were its beautiful, moss-drenched outer islands—Seabrook, Isle of Palms, Sullivan's, Kiawah, Edisto. The people drew me too.

One of my favorite things to do is go to Fischer's Sports Bar & Grill at the Bohicket Marina on Johns Island. There are many fancy dining spots in the Seabrook/Kiawah area, but this is a place for locals, especially the boys who run the charter boats. There is nothing fancy about Fischer's. You can't see the water, and decor is limited to Early Beach, but there is laughter when you enter, the sweet aroma of well-cooked fish, and fresh, cold draft beer. One summer evening fishermen told great yarns about the day's gulfstream catch—mahi-mahis that wouldn't stop and that giant blue marlin they missed.

A spot at the bar opened—sometimes if it's busy I whip behind the bar and help—and sitting there was one Mason H. Dorsey. One of the last survivors of D-Day and the Battle of the Bulge, Mickey was given the French Legion of Honor in Normandy. "It sure quieted down there since December 6, 1945," he once told me. Mickey is in his high eighties and in great shape. He played football at Clemson and I at South Carolina, so he would always muse about the Tigers and the Gamecocks, though lately not as much. Tonight he was holding court about the war in Afghanistan and mentioned more than once if his boss, Gen. George Patton, could take the Third Army over there, it would be over in a month. I believed him.

Then the one and only Sidi Limehouse walked in. There is no character in the South Carolina lowcountry better known than Sidi, a seventy-five-year-old former state assemblyman who looks like a cross between a skinny Grizzly Adams and Andrew Jackson. With a full beard, hair that hasn't been cut since Vietnam, and clothes worn in the fields at his Rosebank Farms on Johns Island, Sidi is a true piece of coastal lore.

"Goin' up to Larry's place and help him plant corn Monday," Sidi said, referencing my neighbor Bradham. "Wanna go?" As much fun as that would be, I don't want to go to a farm in Manning when I have the Atlantic Ocean in sight. More locals pile in, and between Sidi and Mickey, the entertainment continues.

Fischer's is run by Josh Kennedy, a giant of a man with a grand smile. The restaurant is my grandchildren's favorite. Julia Child would flip, as would the surgeon general, if they saw one of Fischer's specialties. Cheese fries are golden brown French fries covered in melted cheese, bacon, and a white sauce known only to a few. Everybody who has been to Fischer's, from the governor to Danny Ford, has had one or more of their cheese fries. The next morning you need liposuction to lose that five pounds you gained.

This part of the world is so different from the starched, formal city of Charlotte, where I've lived for about fifty years. People on this lowcountry pearl are laid-back. They take life as easy as an old dog on an AC vent in August.

The dead of winter appeals to me most. There's a certain feeling after visitors are gone, a softness to it all. On Johns Island, Ole Jones hobbles down Main Road and makes his winter appearance. He's too old to know himself, and a terrible orthopedic injury that wasn't taken care of causes him to shuffle along, his right foot dragging.

"I thanks ye again," he says as I give him a lift to Highway 17. "De Lawd he done grant me 'nother day and I ain't a-complaining. I gots to see my sistah. She gots me some honey she raised and maybe a little lunch. She makes them collards and cornbread when she knows I'm a-coming."

Unlike some on these islands, Ole Jones has seen other places. At sixteen his daddy put him on a shrimp boat to Florida. Saint Augustine had flash and a fort older than Fort Sumter. But it mainly had Doris—short, skinny, pretty. "She done a numbah on me," he said. Ole Jones kept up with Doris through his time in the army during World War II, even as he marveled at the first "Eye Talian" he met and the "raviolee" he ate. In France he was shot in the hip by a German. "Still pains me," he says.

Ole Jones came home, started back shrimping, and married Doris in her AME Zion Church. They were married fifty-six years and had seven children, twenty-five grandchildren, and nine great-grands. "Doris died last year and we buried her right on Johns Island. I do miss that woman, 'cause she was a great cook. My daughters and sistah cook like she did for the most part. Right now I jest live for my chillun and grands and to catch a little fish once in a while, 'cause I am a good fry cook."

It was the last time I saw Ole Jones.

I learned a lesson from Ole Jones, and so does everybody who frequents these islands. The natives are a polite, gracious, and very patient people who take us visitors as we come. After life in the fast lane, it is a welcome repose to turn off busy I-26 and hit Main Road with its huge live oaks festooned with long-hanging moss. Sometimes I imagine, as I drive down that shadowy road, that it's the nineteenth century and I'm in a two-horse carriage. Surely Edgar Allan Poe will pull along beside me and offer me a hand-rolled Cuban cigar. ☽

David Lauderdale

☽

This Isn't a Golf Hole

My favorite spot in South Carolina juts into what writers call the "watery fingers" of Calibogue Sound.

By the time I get there, a good 120 strokes are penciled by my name on the scorecard. But on the tee box of the eighteenth hole at Harbour Town Golf Links in my hometown of Hilton Head Island, trifles like that scatter with the wind.

Brown pelicans with beaks the size of bateaux dive-bomb into a lagoon behind our foursome. Snowy egrets glide over Spartina grass in the salt marsh. A sailboat quietly cuts through waves as Daufuskie Island slumbers across the wide water. Beyond the golf hole that seems so far away stands a red-and-white striped lighthouse at the mouth of a marina.

"It is designed to be played in four strokes," Atlanta columnist Furman Bisher wrote after standing in this spot when Harbour Town Golf Links opened in 1969. "Actually, there is only one way to get there when the wind is presiding. You call a cab."

I'm not thinking about cabs or golf. I'm thinking this spot was pulled from thin air and pluff mud to tug at my heart, not produce bogeys and birdies.

It's true that when Arnold Palmer stood at this spot late on a Sunday afternoon in 1969, he hit a golf shot heard 'round the world. It almost went into the marsh, but one of the most popular figures in American life was about to win his first tournament in fourteen months. That was Harbour Town's first professional tournament, now called the RBC Heritage Presented by Boeing. It put Hilton Head on the map. It helped tourism eventually outdistance textiles as the state's top industry.

The famed eighteenth hole at Harbour Town Golf Links. Courtesy of the Sea Pines Resort. Photograph by Rob Tipton.

But as I squint into the clouds, hoping to see an osprey, I tell my friends, "This isn't a golf hole."

They look at me funny. The sun warms our faces as we wait our turn, and my mind wanders.

I think about Hideo Sasaki.

Sasaki had been interned in Arizona during World War II but grew up to pioneer the concept of collaborative, interdisciplinary landscape architecture to include history, culture, and the environment. He was a young man when a boyish southerner in white buck shoes strode into his office near Harvard University, rolls of maps under his arm. It was Charles E. Fraser, fresh out of Yale Law School. Fraser's family had just bought several thousand acres of mucky land they had the audacity to call Sea Pines and think that interesting people would come there to rejuvenate and build homes, gardens, and churches. He found a like spirit in Sasaki, who "wanted people to understand the human needs and natural forces that were working in the landscape," it was said half a century later when he died.

Fraser also found a like spirit in Pete Dye, a former insurance salesman who designed his unusual course with an upstart named Jack Nicklaus.

Another soul mate was Robert Marvin of Walterboro, who said landscape architecture is not just planting azaleas.

Peter Walker, one of Sasaki's young associates when the firm was hired to plan Sea Pines, came quickly to the phone when I said two magic words: "Charles Fraser." Walker was busy at the time doing the landscape design for the National September 11 Memorial at Ground Zero.

"Not only was Charlie entrepreneurial, he was theatrical," Walker told me. "He looked for things that reach out and touch people—whether it was a place, a building, a program, aesthetics—anything people could respond to on an emotional level."

Enter the Harbour Town Lighthouse. It was ballyhooed in 1969 as the first lighthouse built in South Carolina in 150 years, but it was never a true lighthouse. The light might come on if you're low on beer, but its role was to give heart to a community where a community did not exist. It was to be a "there" where there was no there.

I think of Charles and Mary Fraser and their two little girls dashing through Europe, scouring for ideas for their marina village. They settled on the influences of Portofino. Mary suggested simple, red rocking chairs at Harbour Town where people could relax and people-watch. She brought ideas for a playground from ones she saw in Harlem.

The Frasers spared a large oak as the marina was built and called it the Liberty Oak. Tourists taking pictures with the lighthouse in the background might be overheard today saying it's where Robert E. Lee surrendered to Grant. Charles Fraser asked a young man to play his guitar under the Liberty Oak on summer evenings. Gregg Russell is still at it almost forty years later, with yesterday's children now bringing their own to the tree.

It's all about the human spirit.

Gregg tells about the night he said to a kid, "Say, podnah. Looks like you lost a flip flop." And the kid says: "No, I didn't! I found one."

I think about the marina turning into the South's greatest party on Saturday night during the Heritage. I can see the Gamecock flag whipping in the wind above Joe Rice's 130-foot yacht, the *Rice Quarters,* proving that this is still a South Carolina party. His law partner, the late Ron Motley, used to bring his even larger yacht, the *Themis,* and peons like me would gawk and try to wrap our pea brains around two South Carolina boys winning a $246-billion tobacco settlement for forty-six states.

I start humming when I think of the small graveyard behind condominiums lining the eighteenth fairway. It's a Gullah cemetery. Its oldest

marker is etched by hand for Susan "Ma Sookie" Williams, a midwife born on Hilton Head in 1861. The Braddock's Point Cemetery is an often-overlooked reminder of how we got to where we are in the lowcountry, with many voices and many contributors, some still barely recognized.

I want my friends to hear Rosa Lee Chisolm, who was buried more recently in the cemetery. She rowed her boat up and down Broad Creek until she was pushing eighty. She sang as she pulled the oars, her life always in tune with the tide, wind, and moon. I said how much I'd love to hear her sing the old spirituals, but her daughter, Elizabeth, said her mom's favorite song was the Ray Charles hit "(Night Time Is) The Right Time."

For some reason, when I met Rosa Lee she thought I had come to regulate her fishing habits. "Don't you tell me how many fish I can tek out dat watah," she boomed. "Only God put fish in dat watah."

I think of the men from Cleveland, Ohio, during their thirtieth annual trip to this spot for a week of golf together. They're sitting on a deck by the eighteenth fairway watching the pinkish-orange sun slip below Daufuskie Island with one last, glorious shout-out to a day well spent. I can see them gathered on the eighteenth green with highballs in one hand

and flip phones in the other, beaming a precious moment back home to a new widow. They scatter a few of their buddy's ashes on this special place jutting into the watery fingers of life.

My friends punch me. "David. David. It's your shot."

I pull a tee from my pocket.

"This is it," I say. "This is it. This is why we live here." ☽

The Best Days of Our Lives

I miss my children's childhood. Some days it is a bruised ache in my chest. Their cotton hair tangled with sea salt, their skin slick with sunblock, their eyes at half-mast with bleary, sun-soaked exhaustion. My littlest, Rusk, would wake up and say every day, "What's next? What are we doing today?" He always wanted to know what might happen next, because to him all of life seemed glorious and full of possibility, and something could always "happen next." I love the adults they are today, of course, but the innocence and palpable, primal need for my presence is gone. Those tender days can feel like a dream, as lasting as one summer—until we step onto Daufuskie Island.

They say there is a curse on Daufuskie, that those who try to develop it will be doomed to failure. The island is saturated with ancient Gullah culture and its charms, and there even are rumored to be ghosts. Stories are whispered and tales told to all those who visit. They come to view the Silver Dew Winery and buy Silver Dew Pottery, to see Chase Allen's metal art and drink a cold beer at Freeport. They come to watch the sunset and eat gumbo at Marshside Mama's, to play a round of golf at Bloody Point, or stay at the haunted lighthouse on Haig Point. My in-laws came to Daufuskie two decades ago—not to visit but to live.

Some places become part of our personal mythology. And what is a myth other than a story where the facts don't matter nearly as much as the truth it imparts? There are geographical places in the world that take on lives of their own in the telling and retelling of our life stories.

All good myths have a beginning, although we often don't know what that is. We come into the story halfway through and call it "our beginning." I hadn't yet seen Daufuskie, yet I knew of it. Right out of college,

Daufuskie domicile. Photograph
courtesy of the author.

as a nurse in Atlanta, I read *The Water Is Wide* long before I knew the
fictional island Yamacraw was an actual place, a real island where Pat
Conroy taught. It was the magical setting for the biographical portrayal of
that tumultuous time in his life. For me this island was a swath of land—
five miles long; two and a half miles wide—seen from Harbour Town on
Hilton Head. It was another lowcountry island with oyster-frosted edges,
willowed out between Calibogue Sound and the sea. It was dense with oak
and pine and had one long strip of putty-colored sand on the ocean side.
A mystery as any island is to me, I marveled at how this amoeba-shaped
mass of land could rise from the water in just the place it was.

Daufuskie had already been partially developed with resorts and neigh-
borhoods when I first visited in 1989. My future in-laws had bought a lot
and wanted to show us the island and the Haig Point development. We
climbed aboard a ferry on Hilton Head, and it all felt very exotic, very
Martha's Vineyard without the cars. I won't forget my first impression,
because it was love at first sight.

As the ferry glided across Calibogue Sound, the first thing that came
into focus was the Haig Point lighthouse, a 1700s structure rumored to be
haunted by a ghost named Maggie. The ferry bounced against the dock,
and I walked onto a swaying metal plankway, which slanted up in the
low tide like a shiny children's slide on a playground. We ambled into
what looked to be the most quintessentially southern setting I had ever
seen, something out of a movie or picture book. The live oak trees laced
with Spanish moss, the brick sidewalk lined with palmetto branches that
rattled in the wind like rain, azalea bushes, gas lanterns. And at the end

Meagan Henry demonstrating the languid art of island living. Photograph courtesy of the author.

of the walkway a house with a wraparound porch: the historic Strachan Mansion, which had been brought over on a barge from St. Simons Island years before.

We didn't spend the night the first time we visited. We merely looked at my in-laws' lot and dreamed of the day they would live there and we could visit—a time that seemed so far away. But not even a year later, my husband, Pat, proposed to me in front of the historic and haunted lighthouse. My in-laws moved there the month our first-born, daughter Meagan, was born. It is on this spit of land where all three of our kids learned to ride bikes, run free. We swam in the pool and in the ocean. We ran along Bloody Point beach, and the kids believed it was "our" beach because no one else was ever there. On this floating piece of land, we held every Henry family gathering. We drove golf carts from one end of the island to the other. Ate shrimp at Freeport and Marshside Mama's.

I remember one summer evening at Marshside Mama's. The sun burned the sky orange and red over Calibogue Sound. Now I know that we didn't know we were smack in the middle of some of the best days of our lives. (How do we ever know? We are too tired to know.) During a game of horseshoes our kids were playing, our five-year-old son decided to run across the middle of the game. That was the time we took the emergency boat ride to Hilton Head for stitches. Thomas's first scar came from Daufuskie; it was definitely not his last.

We bought handmade pottery from the Burns at Silver Dew Pottery, and they let us use the pottery wheel, allowed the kids and cousins to run through their property and roll clay balls in their hands. Chase Allen had just started his iron business, and we would hang out on his porch, talk about his art and why he moved to this small island from North Carolina as a young man. Our first (and only) cat, Fuskie, came from Chase's back porch when a stray cat had a litter of kittens. Our dog, Murphy, had just passed away, and Meagan picked up that kitty, held her tiny fluff of a body, and said, "We have to take her home."

There isn't much about our family that hasn't been infused with the briny, rich aroma of Daufuskie Island. Its pluff mud runs through our veins. During the rest of the year, we lived in Atlanta, where clogged highways, school stress, and complicated schedules dominated our lives. We would mark the calendar and count the days until we could return to South Carolina.

Everything changes; we know that. Impermanence is part of the permanent truth in life. Our kids are grown, or mostly so. Some of the resorts have failed. Buildings have rotted, and new ones have been built. Businesses have come and gone. Yet Daufuskie will always remain the same for us, because it is the *story* of it that we carry around. We might mix up the facts (what year was Thomas hit in the head? when did we get the kitten? how many fish art sculptures did we buy? how many times did we picnic on Bloody Point?), but our truth of the island will never change: despite any rumored curse, Daufuskie is a magical and blessed island, a place willing to offer itself to our family, as to any family who is willing to receive it. It is a tiny island that, for us, became larger in story and meaning than in mileage. ☽

1959 O.D. Pavilion. Watercolor by Becky Stowe. Courtesy of the artist.

Ocean Drive

And O.D.? You can't spell good times without O.D., and good times aplenty were had there. They mound up, a heap of sun-burnished days and moonstruck nights that reign as unforgettable, luminous times.

From *Save the Last Dance for Me,* by Tom Poland

)

This Magic Moment

The Grand Strand gets picked on a lot. High-rise time-shares. Northern tourists packed tattoo-to-tattoo on the beach. A frenzy of giant plaster sharks luring you into minigolf ranges.

To well-heeled Charlestonians, just a mention of the "Redneck Riviera" can conjure a look of revulsion—as if venturing too far up Highway 17 means getting your gullet stuffed with hush puppies while all your cash is converted to arcade tokens.

Myrtle is not a gated community. Myrtle is not muted green and brown. If it were a bird, it would be the male, peacocking in garish red and blue and orange and violet. Like a great pop song, Myrtle challenges everyone to drop the snobbery and move your feet.

Come on, you know you want to.

Summer nights at the O.D. Pavilion, the heat fades and the energy moves off the beach. There's a carnival—the kind where part of the thrill is hoping to God someone tightened all the bolts. Next to the Ferris wheel and Tilt-A-Whirl is the Pavilion itself, a ramshackle building with an ice cream shop and a ticket arcade with Skee-Ball and whack-a-mole. But that could be the Jersey Shore or Panama City or any hyperdeveloped coastline. What makes the O.D. Pavilion magical is how that kiddy arcade slides right into a bar with a plywood dance floor and a DJ playing a Drifters song. The walls are covered with pictures of regulars and a few shrines to shaggers who've passed, their loafers nailed to the wall. The dance floor opens to a porch, which itself opens to a thin row of dunes, and after that the beach, the Atlantic Ocean.

It's the most romantic place in South Carolina, where stomach-churning crushes and the moonlit surf are all tied to a dance, one with

Ocean Drive Pavilion, 2000. Mixed media by Becky Stowe. Courtesy of the artist.

specific steps, with form and structure. The O.D. Pavilion represents a rare moment in history where the Jersey Shore meets Downton Abbey. It's always had this gentle tension between child's play and foreplay, the arcade beside the grown-up dance floor.

"I spent my youth waiting to be old enough to go in there," says my friend Donna Logan. A schoolteacher in Charleston, she grew up a short drive inland in Mullins. "When I was little and we would go to that arcade, I would always look at the dancers on the dance floor. Once I hit high school, we went every time we could."

My wife and I first started going to Myrtle when we were engaged. It was a cheap thrill in the winter. Then, in the early 2000s, you could rent an oceanfront room for $25 and get breakfast for $1.99. Coming as we did from constrained Charleston, with the insular circles you're meant to aspire to, Myrtle's screaming billboards were a friendly welcome.

We went back again for our first anniversary. The blue Astroturf of the Court Capri hotel was no longer up to our standards, so we stayed at Camelot by the Sea, where a man dressed as a medieval squire edified us on the complexities of the accommodations.

"What are your rates?" I asked.

"We have thirty-six different types of rooms, ergo, we have thirty-six different rates."

(*Ergo,* used thusly, is now a permanent part of our family lexicon.)

Ten years later, we'd take the kids up to an indoor waterpark in the off-season, hit the pancake houses. (I could go on sabbatical, spend a winter writing at the Omega Pancake House.)

The past few summers we've stayed with family from Burlington, North Carolina, in a condo in North Myrtle, a mile from the dance floor at the O.D. Pavilion. Unfortunately I don't shag. When I took cotillion in the 1980s, it was unheard of for a thirteen-year-old boy at a snide private school to care about much of anything, much less learning a couples dance step.

Later on, in high school, my girlfriend was a ballet and jazz dancer. She would shag with a friend at parties. She never taught me how; I never asked. We broke up freshman year of college.

Still the shag always seemed special, something very Carolina. It was sweet and nostalgic yet still current and cool. In the '80s the baby boomers still held the reins of culture, and they were not a generation looking to bury the glories of their youth. We teenagers might've worn our Sex Pistols or Surf Naked T-shirts, but when the adults drank wine coolers and put on "Sixty Minute Man" or slurred the dirty lyrics to "Louie, Louie," we knew they were privy to some deep-down grown-up stuff we weren't getting yet.

The exact origins of the shag are murky. It most likely developed organically, in several places in the late 1940s and early 1950s. Dancers in the South evolved the jitterbug and the Big Apple into a mellower, silkier step, better suited to hot, crowded dance floors. The emphasis was on the beat and the cool footwork.

The current O.D. Pavilion, built in the mid-1950s, along with Robert's, which it replaced, was one of a cluster of spots around North Myrtle where the shag craze grew. (Since this essay is for a book about places, to be clear, "North Myrtle Beach" is a relatively new one. It wasn't until 1968 that Cherry Grove, Ocean Drive, Windy Hill, and Crescent Beach consolidated into the new town of North Myrtle. Some still refuse to call the beach at the corner of Main Street and Ocean Boulevard anything but "O.D.") Other dance pavilions included the Pad, which Donna Logan says had an "aura of danger"—latticework blocked views of the "dirty shagging"—and Sonny's in Cherry Grove.

"Sonny's was a wooden building with open slats and a wood floor—probably an inch between the boards on the floor, and a fabulous jukebox," Donna says. "It had a very minimal bar, just a couple of coolers, because no one was drinking anything other than P.B.R."

Then as now, it was more about the dancing than the drinking.

"We didn't take lessons," she says. "We learned from each other, and it was very competitive. A guy we called the dancing king, he'd come down from Charlotte each year, and we'd spend the summers trying to learn the new moves he'd worked out."

(To hear a Charleston resident praise anything coming out of my hometown is a rare treat. North and South Carolina are very different, but the shag is one thing that connects us.)

In the 1950s the boys were the "peacocks." Their tailored look was tapered "peg" pants, shirtless V-neck sweaters or oxford shirts, peroxided hair. Donna, a teenager in the 1960s, says girls wore "little ballet flats made by Pappagallo, Bermuda shorts and little short-sleeved collared shirts."

The look has changed. At the S.O.S. (Society of Stranders) Mid-Winter Break in January, the ladies wear loose silk blouses and black pants, the men are in khakis and sweater vests. A constant are the penny loafers or tasseled Bass Weejuns, with leather soles for sliding.

In the winter the sandy dance floor of the Pavilion is closed, and the carnival has packed up and left behind a gray gravel lot. But the other shag clubs, the O.D. Arcade, Duck's, the O.D. Beach Club, the Pirate's Cove, are going strong.

With my wife and kids back in the hotel lazy river, I ventured out alone to check out the S.O.S. Mid-Winter. I was only a few sips into a Budweiser at Fat Harold's when I met Gail Roberson. "This is Spring Break for old people," she said. "We all grew up dancing. It's all we did. This is real dancing. Dancing nowadays is just jumping up and down."

Originally from Virginia, Gail moved to Sunset Beach, North Carolina, in the 1990s. After her husband passed away in 2001, her friends took her dancing one night. She'd danced as a teenager but had never seen the shag.

"The first time I ever saw it, I walked in the door and said, 'I don't know what this is, but I have to learn how to do it.' It changed my life. Once you learn the basic steps, you can do whatever you want."

Not long after that, she moved to North Myrtle to be closer to Fat Harold's. Now she goes out dancing with her new beau twice a week.

It's hard to imagine a place more centered around a particular style of dance. North Myrtle is the Shag Mecca. Shaggers come here the way gamblers go to Vegas or skiers go to Vail. The water tower has a silhouette of shaggers on it. The souvenir shops hawk "Shags Well with Others" tees. At least two stores are dedicated to selling shagging shoes (and beach music CDs).

Stones embedded in the sidewalks commemorate legendary dancers such as "Cadillac Jack" Smith and Betty Lou Hickey Parrott. Fat Harold's has two dance floors with separate DJ booths. Plaques on the wall commemorate the Sugarfoot Shag Club, Shag Atlanta, Boogie on the Bay, and many others from all over the South.

"Back when we were kids, we didn't have these clubs," Gail says. "We danced in beer joints, honky-tonks. It would be nothing to be dancing and have a beer bottle fly by your head. Here, there are never any arguments, no altercations, no one's overly drunk. People are just here to be happy."

The charm of South Carolina is its casual elegance. And as the DJ plays an Embers tune and the dance floor fills with that slippery, smooth shuffle step, you'll never see anything more casually elegant.

Granted, the dancers are getting older. They're still light on their feet but not as light on the scale. Donna recalled a recent Sonny's reunion at the Pavilion. A lot of the guys still had moves that were "intimidating," but "one of them had to change his shirt five times."

You have to wonder if the shag may be nearing the end of a good, long run.

"It will last as long as people have feet," Donna counters. She often gets Facebook videos of friends' children and grandchildren shagging.

So hopefully the Pavilion and Fat Harold's and the others are going to be around for a long while, maybe forever. But still, go soon, if you can.

What's the matter, your shoes nailed to the wall? ♪

Zen Surfer

Like many life-changing events, this one happened quite by accident.

It was during the spring of 1970, not long after my sixteenth birthday. Some friends and I had driven the sixty-eight miles from our hometown of Dillon to Ocean Drive in North Myrtle Beach. We were hanging around the O.D. Pavilion, shooting pool, checking out girls, and enjoying a taste of grown-up freedom.

I loved the beach. The sun, salt in the air, and sound of the surf seemed to amplify this newfound freedom, and I was feeling a mixture of contentment and teenage cockiness as I walked across Main Street to McElveen's Drug Store for a lemonade.

McElveen's was on the corner of Main and Ocean Boulevard, and they made the best lemonade in the world. Fresh-squeezed lemons, a dash of sugar, and crushed ice. I bought a large, turned to leave, and came to a screeching halt at the magazine rack.

There on the middle shelf was a magazine called *Surfer.* On its cover was a huge ocean wave, backlit by the sun and barreling straight toward me. Tucked inside the wave was a crouching surfer on a foam-and-fiberglass missile. His grin was euphoric, but his outstretched arms and delicate balance gave him the aura of a Zen monk calm in the storm.

I stood there transfixed and wondered how it must feel to ride such a wave. I bought the magazine, hurried back across the street to one of the picnic tables on the pavilion's deck by the beach, and began flipping through the pages as the sun warmed my shoulders. I saw photo after photo of surfers carving long, graceful turns on shimmering walls of water, standing on the nose of their boards while speeding down the faces of translucent waves, and, like the surfer in the cover photo, riding deep inside cascading aqua tunnels. Engrossed in one such photo, I felt a presence at my shoulder. A guy about my age with long, sun-bleached hair, puka-shell necklace, and faded T-shirt was gazing down at the magazine.

"Nice bowl," he said.

"Nice what?" I said, squinting up at him.

"Nice bowl. Tube. Barrel. Green room. I wish we got waves like that around here."

"Wait a minute," I said. "Are you saying people do this around here?"

"Sure, man. We don't get waves anything like that, but you can get fun little rides at the pier all the time. You should check it out. Good talkin' to you. I gotta scoot."

With that, he bounded off the deck, over the dunes, and started walking north on the beach toward the Tilghman Fishing Pier, which was named after the longtime local family who owned it.

I felt a pied piper pull to follow him. Could there really be surfers in South Carolina? Actual surfing down the beach from where I was sitting? My friends were inside the pavilion shooting pool and playing pinball, and I yelled I would see them later. I crossed Main Street, walked down the sidewalk past an open-air bar called the Beach Party, turned left toward the pier, and was there in no time.

Standing on the beach just north of the pier, I gazed out at the ocean, and sure enough, half a dozen surfers were bobbing up and down while sitting on their surfboards about a hundred yards offshore. I needed a better angle to see, so I scurried over the dunes, across the parking lot, through the pier's bait shop and game room, and out on the long old collection of boards, beams, and timbers.

I sat on one of the benches and watched as a set of waves appeared and began to roll steadily toward the shore. The waves were much smaller than the ones in the magazine, but nevertheless the surfers all dropped to a prone position on their boards and began to paddle toward them. One surfer was farther out than the rest, and he let the first two weaker swells roll under him. Then he turned and paddled effortlessly into the third wave. He sprang to his feet, turned off the bottom of the wave as it broke behind him, and flew down the face, making all the right adjustments to maintain his speed.

He was streaking straight toward the pier, and I held my breath as he made one last, spray-inducing turn and sailed up and over the back of the wave directly below me, a mere ten feet from a barnacled piling. I was mesmerized, hooked like a king mackerel by one of the old fishermen at the pier's end. From that moment on, I wanted to be a surfer. I wanted to feel the speed and the spray and the quiet calm of these surfers, now paddling lazily back out to wait for another wave.

And so my quest began. I didn't realize it then, but the Tilghman Fishing Pier and the two hundred yards of beach and ocean to its north would become a holy place for me, a surfing Mecca I would return to again and again. It was where I began a journey that would become as spiritual as it was physical.

My first surfboard came from a high school buddy who said I could have the board his older brother left in their garage. It turned out to be the size of a battleship and often threatened to decapitate me after wipeouts. Later that summer, after saving $120 from mowing neighborhood lawns, I bought my first surfboard at Ocean Surf Shop in Myrtle Beach. I picked out a six-foot Sunshine model, blue and red and absolutely beautiful in my eyes. I also bought a puka-shell necklace and a pair of Birdwell Beach Britches, thus achieving more credibility than the cutoff jeans I'd been surfing in. I had the artifacts, but I still needed some skills.

Surfing didn't come easy for me. I struggled with the timing of catching a wave, coming to my feet once I'd actually caught one, and maintaining my balance throughout the ride. I envied the more accomplished surfers who paddled easily past me and showered me with spray from their hard, precise turns. But not once did they make me feel unwanted. I was welcomed into their fold, encouraged, and advised. Gradually I began to figure out the best time to turn and paddle into a wave. I became a stronger paddler, and my balance improved. I was making turns down the face of the wave, and learned to "cut out" at the end of a ride instead of jumping off my board.

I also learned to read the tides, winds, and swell direction. When I wasn't in the water, I was on the pier watching the movement of the ocean and noting where the best waves broke during certain conditions. I would learn surfers called this "becoming a true waterman." I had miles to paddle and many waves to catch before I would consider myself a competent surfer, but by the end of that summer in 1970, I felt like I was on my way.

For the next few years, I went surfing every chance I got. The summers were magical. Hot sand on the dunes gave way to cool water as I darted from the pier's parking lot to the ocean. The air was filled with the scent of coconut tanning oil, orange-flavored surf wax, and salty sea breezes. My buddies and I would surf all morning, then walk to a pool room on Main

Street called the Sports Center, where we devoured chili cheeseburgers the size of hubcaps and washed them down with bottles of Coca-Cola.

As much as I loved summer at the beach, I came to love fall and winter even more. The tourists had all gone home, the waves were generally larger due to "nor'easters," and surfers were given free range to ride the waves anywhere along the beach. Sure, the water was colder, but that just meant we wore wetsuits and enjoyed not having to dodge swimmers in the shore break.

Ocean Drive became a quiet little town in winter. The local population was small, and the only visitors were surfers and fishermen. (This was before a multitude of golf courses arrived with their year-round deals enticing snowbirds to the beach all year.) The surfing population thinned out too, and whenever I pulled in at the pier, I could immediately tell who was in the water just by the vehicles in the parking lot.

Dedicated surfers from many towns migrated to the pier in wintertime, and I got to know quite a few. Surfers from Marion and Loris in South Carolina. Shallotte and Tabor City in North Carolina. We became an extended family of wave riders, and we laughed and surfed and loved our laidback lifestyle. It was a time of no worries, no fear, and no pressure. We felt like we'd live forever.

Surfing had become the most important thing in my life, and I started making big decisions based on my desire to ride the waves. I graduated from high school in 1972 and chose to attend college in Charleston to be close to the surf at Folly Beach and Isle of Palms. When the old Volkswagen Fastback I'd been driving was about to bite the dust, I found a hippie chick on James Island who wanted to sell her VW bus that came with a double bed inside, curtains, and an icebox. I was in love (with the bus, not the chick), and it became my home on wheels, delivering me to wherever good waves were breaking.

For surfers in the Southeast, that meant two places: the central Atlantic coast of Florida and the Outer Banks of North Carolina. Thanks to my trusty bus, I made many trips to both, testing myself in larger, more powerful waves. I flunked those tests more than I'd like to admit, but the effort was always enriching.

Still I returned to the old Tilghman Pier in Ocean Drive, not because the waves were smaller and more forgiving but because it felt like home. I would spend the night in my bus in the parking lot, crawl out at dawn, walk over the sand dunes, and check the waves. Sitting on the pier drinking

Rhythm. Graphite and watercolor by Rob Barge. Courtesy of the artist.

coffee as the sun came up over the ocean and listening to the quiet thump of the waves always filled me with that Zen-like calm I'd perceived in the surfer on that old magazine cover.

In the 1980s I attended graduate school at the University of South Carolina in Columbia and earned a master's degree in journalism. I took a job at the afternoon newspaper, the *Columbia Record,* in 1986 and began a career as a newspaper writer. But I still made weekend surfing trips to Ocean Drive, and every fall I took a week's vacation in North Carolina to surf at Cape Hatteras—my VW bus giving way to a four-wheel-drive Mitsubishi, just the vehicle for bouncing over coastal sand dunes.

I was on one of those surf safaris to the Outer Banks in September 1989 when I began to hear frightening weather reports from farther south. A hurricane was headed up the coast, and it was big. I had been enjoying better than average waves, but knew if I stayed too long an evacuation notice would be issued and I'd be sitting in a long line of traffic. So I left early and made it back to Columbia on Friday, September 22, the night Hurricane Hugo came ashore in Charleston.

It was a whopper, with sustained winds of 140 miles per hour that extended 45 miles from the storm's center. I rode it out in Columbia, where Hugo was powerful enough to blow down trees and knock out power 114 miles inland. I knew the beaches had taken a terrible pounding, and as reports came in, I learned of vast destruction along the coast.

Many South Carolina fishing piers were obliterated, including the old Tilghman Pier on Ocean Drive. It was like a punch in the gut. Although I didn't surf there as much as I used to, I still felt like I'd lost an old friend. I hoped a new pier would be constructed where so many young surfers could experience the same magic I had. But while nearby piers at Garden City, Crescent Beach, and Cherry Grove were rebuilt, the Tilghman Pier was never reconstructed. It was heartbreaking for me and many other surfers, too.

Over the years many more changes came to Ocean Drive. Gone are the Beach Party and McElveen's Drug Store. Huge, high-rise resorts overlook the ocean. Four-lane highways lead to Ocean Drive and Cherry Grove, and more people live at the beach year round.

Yet even now, when I stand on the beach near where the old pier once stood, I can close my eyes and hear it creak and moan as waves wrap around its pilings. I hear Santana's "Oye Como Va" coming from the jukebox in the game room and smell the fruity scent of slightly melted surf wax as surfers lean their boards against its railings.

Then I open my eyes and see two young surfers walking by with boards under their arms, heading up the beach to where a sandbar is producing some nice little waves about seventy-five yards offshore.

"Rip it up," I say, and they grin and give me the "hang loose" hand sign. I grin back and at that moment, I know all is right in the world. ☺

Adluh. Acrylic by Blue Sky. Courtesy of Blue Sky Studio.

Still Standing

Since 1961 Gervais Street in Columbia has been dominated by one single thing—the 120-foot neon sign for Adluh Flour. Unchanging in its blinking on-again, off-again rhythm, the sign represents South Carolina's sole surviving mill, a family operation that's been grinding out corn and flour for more than a hundred years. Adluh's slogan is "Same Today, Same Always." That's strong comfort for the restaurants, grocers, and home cooks who've favored Adluh products since its beginnings in 1900.

As Gervais Street shifted from seedy and scary to expensive and chic, Adluh and its iconic sign remained. Employees work in a building listed on the National Register of Historic Properties, where they produce the South Carolina state flour, as declared by the state's agriculture department in 1994. Adluh stands behind its mixes and breaders, grits and flour. Adluh recipes, they say, are nothing short of "table-tested."

This recipe is from Jack Edgerton Jr. (1948–2015), a third-generation Adluh employee whose grandfather John Bennett Allen Sr. started the company.

Jack's Crock Pot White Cheese Grits

1 cup Adluh Stone-Ground White Grits (may also use yellow grits)
3 cups water, hot
1 cup milk, heavy cream, or half-and-half (may use just water)
Pinch salt

Pinch sugar
¼ stick margarine
¾ cup cheese, shredded
1–2 teaspoons Texas Pete hot sauce

Add hot water to crock pot that is set on high and then add grits. Cook on high, stirring every 15–20 minutes. After 1 ½ to 2 hours, add milk or cream and continue stirring. Wait 30–40 minutes, then add cheese and hot sauce. Add margarine, sugar, and salt/bullion at any time. Reduce heat and simmer until ready to serve. Lid should be kept on pot during the entire cooking cycle. The longer they cook, the better they taste!

Makes 4–6 servings.

When first adding grits to hot water, stir and remove floating particles (corn bran) with a ladle or spoon if desired. Cooking time can be reduced or increased depending on the consistency desired. Recipe can be doubled or tripled to fit the cooking container size. For standard grits, omit the cheese and hot sauce.

Hotel Resilience

Before it was rescued and transformed into the resplendent site it is today, the Poinsett Hotel nearly perished. "The jewel of downtown Greenville" survived the Great Depression, bankruptcy, urban blight of the 1970s and 1980s, mattress-burning vagrants, rot and mildew, and—as rumor has it—devil worshipers.

Today, as I write this, I am sitting in the hotel's piano bar, one of the most romantic spots in Greenville. Here, from the comfort of an over-stuffed chair, one can listen to a pianist playing jazz on the baby grand while admiring the mosaic tile floors, marble stairways, and decorative plaster, lovingly restored. These days it's not hard to imagine how the Poinsett looked in 1925, the year it opened. What is harder to believe is that until early 1990, the Poinsett Hotel was considered one of the eleven most endangered historical sites in South Carolina.

When I was in high school, "dragging Main Street" in a caravan of cars was a popular pastime. But you never got out of the car. That was dangerous. The Poinsett, with its boarded-up windows, looked haunted. The hint of ruined finery—torn wallpaper and ragged drapes, cracked plaster—added an air of poignancy. Like Miss Emily's dilapidated manse in William Faulkner's story "A Rose for Emily," the building appeared to be "lifting its stubborn and coquettish decay above the cotton wagons and the gasoline pumps—an eyesore among eyesores." Who could believe that decades before, the Poinsett's guests had included Amelia Earhart, John Barrymore, Cornelius Vanderbilt, Bobby Kennedy, and Liberace?

My mother worked at the Poinsett Hotel the summer of her senior year in high school to earn money for college. It was 1961, a pivotal year for the hotel, the point at which it teetered before plunging into rack and

Grand banquet at the Poinsett Hotel, Greenville. Photograph courtesy of the Greenville County Historical Society.

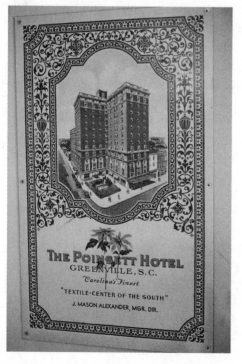

Vintage poster. Photograph courtesy of Sposa Bella Photography.

The Poinsett in 2015. Photograph courtesy of Sposa Bella Photography.

ruin. Mason Alexander, known in the South and beyond as one of the best managers in the hotel business, had just retired from the Poinsett. "Old Admiral Spit and Polish," as he was known, had managed the hotel for thirty years with a "philosophy of four Cs": cleanliness, cooking, competence, and courtesy.

My mother laundered money—so to speak. Mason Alexander had a thing for clean money. She washed coins in a special machine with liquid soap. And every morning someone would bring crisp bills from the bank. Whoever stayed or dined in the Poinsett left with clean money—and everyone in town knew it.

My mother worked in the office. "I had an excellent typing teacher and beat out my best friend for the job," she said. "I just typed faster." Her father would drop her off in the mornings, and she would walk down the long hall by the shoeshine man. The aroma of spoonbread, one of the hotel's signature foods, filled the air. Sometimes my mother worked in "marketing," distributing brochures about the hotel, traveling as far as Charlotte to hand out information.

The uniform she was instructed to wear was a dress—a little too short—but it was for work. Never mind that her Southern Baptist parents did not allow her to wear Bermuda shorts. This was for work—an office job—and that trumped my grandmother's Victorian sensibilities about clothing. "I remember trying to be beguiling at a convention in Charlotte to attract customers for conventions at the Poinsett," my mother said. "I remember they wanted me to dress up."

But even the best marketing and most beguiling southern belles couldn't save the Poinsett from what was coming: in the 1960s the motel industry boomed, while city hotels closed. The Poinsett was sold and became a retirement home in the 1970s. In 1986 the hotel was foreclosed, and by the end of that year, the last residents of the retirement home moved out. The hotel stood empty. Those were the grim, dark years—when vagrants burned mattresses in the hotel, when a nearby storeowner was quoted in the newspaper as saying candles, beheaded dolls, and blood from pigeons inside the lobby was a sign that Satan worshippers had taken up residence.

But then—my favorite part. The happy ending. In November 1997 developers of the historic Francis Marion Hotel in Charleston purchased the Poinsett, and the $20 million renovation began. The Westin Poinsett reopened for business in October 2000. Today it is gorgeous and bustling, with tourists filling its rooms and brides and debutantes dancing again in its ballroom. That's what I love about the place—its tenacity, from ruin to luxury, from riches to rags to riches. The Westin Poinsett Hotel—she's one tough broad. ☾

)

A Nineteenth-Century Poet's Garden Bower

> While yesterevening, through the vale
> Descending from my cottage door
> I strayed, how cool and fresh a look
> All nature wore.

So reads the first stanza of "Haw-Blossoms," composed by the twenty-three-year-old James Mathewes Legare in 1846. The poet had just arrived in Aiken that year to take up residence in a two-room, wood-framed house at the bottom of Laurens Street. Though additions were made to the original floor plan by succeeding residents, the cottage still stands surrounded by greenery, low shrubbery like the hawthorn bushes described in the poem and overhanging trees both in front and in the side garden to the left of the house as it faces the street.

The fact that his new home was located on what was then the edge of town, next to an extensive wooded area, must have been a comfort to Legare (pronounced *Le-gree*), who had relocated with his parents—his father, John, was hired as the municipal postmaster—largely because of Aiken's reputation as a health resort. Especially for those, like Legare, suffering from respiratory problems, the town's higher elevation, relatively dry air, and restorative springs offered the hope of a healthier life.

Thus the family endured the ten-hour train trip from Charleston—Aiken was one of several towns that were established a little more than a decade earlier when the first railroad crossed the state—and young Legare set about planning his future. My own arrival in Aiken some 40 years ago, exactly 130 years after Legare's, was not by train but by car; but I imagine

This portrait of Legare appeared in *The Knicker-bocker Gallery* (New York, 1855).

that we shared much the same sense of possibility. My path was more defined than his since I had accepted a tenure-track position at the local university, but I can only assume that starry-eyed ambition motivated us both.

Imagine my excitement, as a specialist in nineteenth-century American literature, when I discovered that a minor poet of that period had lived and worked in Aiken! During his twelve years in the Laurens Street cottage, which he called home until his death at thirty-five, Legare wrote the short volume by which he is remembered today. *Orta Undus,* roughly translated as "sprung from waves" and generally considered to be a reference to the birth of Venus, contains poems primarily on the two subjects for which the goddess is principally associated, love and beauty.

Love Legare found in the form of his future wife, Anne, who was for a time a student of his in a painting class he had established in a two-room studio built in 1850 next to the cottage—this structure was later connected by subsequent residents to the left side of the main house. Beauty he sought principally in nature. The poets of the Romantic movement reverenced the curative power of nature; by exercising the imagination in a natural setting, they believed that an individual could transcend his everyday troubles and find a consolation of sorts. How attractive that belief must have been to Legare, whose health problems and genteel poverty were lingering burdens!

It was not long after I took up my teaching duties that I started to introduce some of Legare's verse into the curriculum, especially the upper-division course in American Romanticism. His poems follow the typical pattern established by such giants as Wordsworth, Coleridge, and Keats: the speaker's engagement with some aspect of nature eventually leads to a revelation about life. I thought my students would more readily tackle the material of the course if they discovered that a poetic practitioner of the Romantic stripe had once lived in their own town. Thus we read a handful of Legare poems that touch upon the flora of this part of the state, including "To Jasmines in December," "The Laurel Blossom," and "A May Morn."

In my personal resuscitation of the poet's work, I was following in the footsteps of another scholastic Aikenite of an earlier generation. For roughly twenty years (1921–1942), led by the school librarian Elizabeth Teague, the members of the now-defunct Legare Literary Society at Aiken High collected money to erect a granite monument over the poet's heretofore unmarked grave in the churchyard of Saint Thaddeus Episcopal Church. In the same plot are buried his parents and wife. This gesture has always touched me. That someone would care enough about the life and work of a largely ignored local poet to spark the cooperation of her students in a collective effort to mark his grave is absolutely splendid.

Over the years I have had many occasions to summon up, both in the classroom and out, the memory of James Mathewes Legare and his Aiken residency. One recent undergraduate research project I supervised, for example, involved photographing specimens of furniture embellished with plastic cotton decoration in storage at the Charleston Museum. In order to make his mark, Legare tried his hand at poetry, painting, and invention. His keynote scientific discovery was what he called lignine, or plastic cotton. By a chemical process of his own devising, he converted common cotton fiber into a substance that could be dyed, molded, and worked into a variety of shapes. For a time Legare thought it would make his fortune; but a lack of interest on the part of local investors dashed those dreams. Still the furniture pieces, now in varying stages of disrepair and rarely on public view, engaged the imagination of my student-photographer, who told me later that he felt like a scholar-adventurer stumbling across a hidden treasure trove.

Legare-Morgan Cottage. Graphite drawing by Michael Budd. Courtesy of the artist.

In my own published work—two of my books feature chapters on Legare—I have often had occasion to consider the challenges he faced as an author. Like me he had his own friendly arguments with editors. In a footnote to one of the poems printed in *Orta Undis,* for example, he acknowledges the fact that the work in question first appeared in *Putnam's Monthly* in a slightly different form. The difference, we soon discover, was the result of the fact that the editor took it upon himself to change the poet's text. While asserting a "modest preference for his unaided composition," Legare goes on to ask the reader if the editor's "novel literary powers" have "exceeded his ability as far as he has his function of editor." Any writer who has disagreed with an editor's amendments to his original composition will sympathize with poor Legare.

The cottage itself has also played a role in my professional and personal life. For a time the building was operated as a restaurant, and USC-Aiken would host dinners for visiting writers there. It seemed entirely appropriate that the erstwhile residence of one writer would serve as the site for celebrating the work of other individuals dedicated to the literary arts.

Now the house is rental property, but it is my hope that its status on the National Register of Historic Places will keep it safe for future generations.

There are far grander houses in Aiken, including some of the mansions built during its heyday as a winter resort, but none is as old—some estimate that the central portion of the Legare-Morgan Cottage dates to 1837, just two years after the city's founding—and none has such poignant associations. ☽

Bernard E. Powers Jr.

)

"More than a House"

I have frequently driven the twelve miles northwest of downtown Charleston along the scenic tree-lined Ashley River Road leading to Drayton Hall, one of America's premier historic sites. Here along the banks of the Ashley River are revealed some of the nation's most crucial stages, including the colonial era and Revolutionary War, the antebellum rice and cotton South, the Civil War, Reconstruction, and the birth of a New South in the late nineteenth and early twentieth centuries. The "great house" of Drayton Hall is the centerpiece of what was once an extensive collection of plantation buildings situated on 350 acres. This formidable estate, which the *South Carolina Gazette* observed resembled a "Palace and Gardens," was home to seven generations of Draytons, beginning in 1738 until its sale to the National Trust for Historic Preservation in 1974. The two-story portico made the residence unique in the British colonies in the mid-eighteenth century, and it remains one of the most important examples of Georgian Palladian architecture preserved in America today. Despite its well-established architectural bona fides, the maxim of the staff at Drayton Hall is that the site is "more than a house." At first glance a visitor might wonder how this could be.

When taking a guided tour, as I frequently have, as the group approaches the residence's grand entrance, the docent explains the characteristics of Palladian architecture, illustrating how the size, placement, and number of windows and doors reflect the symmetry and balance of the form. There are further illustrations inside the building as the tour winds through rooms grand and small. The discussion about symmetry piqued my interest as an African American and a historian of the black experience. In my earliest visit, more than two decades ago, the grandeur of the

Drayton Hall, Charleston. Courtesy of the Drayton Hall Preservation Trust. Photograph by Charlotte Caldwell.

Draytons' lives was clearly evident, but little if anything was mentioned about the black and enslaved majority of its residents. It was possible to tour the house and learn only a partial story of Drayton Hall. I naturally pondered the asymmetries of plantation life embodied in the lives of the enslaved Africans and their descendants. "If these walls could speak," I wondered, "what information would they yield, what secrets would disgorge?"

All my academic training and instincts told me that slaveholding was such a crucial component in the lives of families such as the Draytons that they could not be understood without knowing something about those they owned. This house seemed like the best place for observing the intimate interconnections between black and white lives, yet there was silence. Then I saw it: the well-worn spiral service stairwell that begins in the raised English basement and reaches the upper floors, even opening into the bedchambers. As it was traversed by slaves, its partially obscured location in the inner core of the house speaks to their proximate and subordinate yet essential presence at the heart of its operation. Winding upward, the stairwell's circular movement is emblematic of the way black and white, slave and free shared tightly entwined lives, drawn together by the South's "peculiar institution." This visual was a compelling argument for including black lives in the overall plantation narrative.

Fortunately over the past few decades, with varying degrees of success, historic sites have been grappling with the African American experience. Drayton Hall has been among the leaders in the process. As executive director Dr. George McDaniel and his staff reviewed their interpretive plans, I was one among many whose opinions and suggestions were solicited. Over the years they have tried different strategies and capitalized on their unique resources to give the visitor a more sophisticated understanding of black and white life here and also how historical issues of race and place reverberate down to the present.

If the truth be told, there are too many African Americans today who are embarrassed by a history of enslavement. Many, especially outside the South, also believe that once freedom came, the freedmen severed all connection with their old plantations. Drayton Hall tells a more complex story, one that is particularly fascinating in the way it incorporated the descendants of African people living at the site both before and after Emancipation. There is a deep-seated pride of place instilled by earlier generations. For some the reason was based on a long sentimental attachment to the place. For example, the Bowens family oral tradition indicates that the earliest Bowens ancestor in South Carolina arrived with the Draytons from Barbados. For others that pride resulted from the tightly knit freedmen's communities on the site after the Civil War, which allowed some to avoid sharecropping by working in the new phosphate industry. This identification with Drayton Hall has been of great benefit, because the modern-day descendants have contributed to the site in invaluable ways.

Richmond Bowens was its earliest interpreter of the African American experience. The grandson of an antebellum enslaved man, Bowens was born on the property in 1908 and worked at Drayton Hall until the Great Depression caused his departure for employment. Upon his return in 1974, he worked as an interpreter, and his experiences brought incomparable authenticity to his work. From the front of the museum shop, Bowens answered visitors' questions and eagerly shared personal reminiscences and stories about Drayton Hall handed down through the generations. This was an avocation for him, and his memories, preserved in taped interviews, have proved invaluable for reconstructing African American life. Richmond Bowens also took steps to pass the stories about this site to relatives, particularly those who resided in the area, and he encouraged them to maintain contact with Drayton Hall. He continued his work until

1997, when he fell ill and passed away the following year. He is buried on the property in the African American cemetery.

My special appreciation for life at Drayton Hall resulted from meeting Richmond Bowens's cousins, Rebecca Campbell and Catherine Braxton. Their grandfather, Willis Johnson, was born at Drayton Hall after the Civil War. Although he and his wife, Rebecca, moved to Charleston in the early twentieth century, they frequently took their family to visit Bowens's relatives at Drayton Hall. Visiting there was an important family tradition passed on to Rebecca and Catherine, and it strengthened when cousin Richmond returned. Since then the two sisters have contributed much to Drayton Hall through their own personal stories and genealogical knowledge. Catherine proclaims, "This place matters; if not to anybody else, it matters to me because it involves my ancestors that left a legacy here." That legacy is a material one, because African people were among the builders of the great house. That legacy also was deeply spiritual, and Rebecca and Catherine credit their ancestors as the source of their values and ideals.

To honor that past and show a commitment to present and future generations of descendants, Drayton Hall refurbished the property's African American cemetery and integrated it into its overall interpretive plan. In late 2007 the African American Memorial Steering Committee was formed, consisting of Drayton Hall staff, community representatives, scholars, and Philip Simmons Foundation representatives as well as Bowens and Drayton family members. I joined the committee, which is how I met Catherine and Rebecca.

The cemetery is on a ten-acre plot off the main entry road and dates to the 1790s, making it among America's oldest functioning cemeteries. Bowens was interred there in 1998. Headstones were few, because most early graves had wooden markers that deteriorated long ago. Nor were the graves organized in neat linear rows. Trees, shrubs, and native plants were interspersed throughout the site. Bowens had said the cemetery always looked this way, and one of his wishes was that it be left in a natural state. When asked about caring for those interred there, he famously said, "Leave 'em rest." Based on his recollections, the committee decided against formal landscaping.

The committee also decided to use an iron structure to frame the entrance to the cemetery formed by a natural break in the trees. The form of the structure was uncertain: should it be a gate or an arch? We finally decided an arch would reflect traditional African and African American ideas of spirituality most accurately. Gates suggested hard and fast borders:

A Sacred Place: The African American Cemetery at Drayton Hall. Courtesy of the Drayton Hall Preservation Trust. Photograph by John Apsey.

an archway conveyed permeability and the informal relationship between the material and the spiritual, the living and the dead. The late Philip Simmons, the renowned Charleston blacksmith, designed much of the arch, but because of his age and failing health, Ronnie Pringle, one of his cousins, completed the design, fabrication, and installation. At the apex of the archway and contained within its metallic borders are the words "Leave 'Em Rest." A cross rests above these words, atop the center.

On October 9, 2010, this area, now called "A Sacred Place: The African American Cemetery at Drayton Hall," was formally dedicated. There were songs and personal reflections of black and white Drayton Hall descendants and Dr. Lonnie Bunch, director of the National Museum of African American History and Culture, gave the keynote address, marking the event's national significance. The most moving part occurred when Lorraine White and Corey Furtick led a procession of 150–200 people to the memorial archway with a duet rendition of "Wade in the Water." With their melodious voices reverberating through the woods to guide them, a heterogeneous group of blacks and whites, young and old, attired in styles ranging from African garb to suits and dresses, marched silently forward, two by two, each bearing a flower they placed at the base of the arch or atop the earthen depressions of the graves. Then the list of names was read one after the other, totaling hundreds. Most were single Christian names like Billy or Diane, denoting enslaved people. There were also names like Monday and Quash, suggesting African origins, and Fatimah and Ishmael, suggesting Islamic influence. The contemporary vitality of African culture in the lowcountry was also evidenced when a Gullah blessing of the archway was pronounced and assembled onlookers affirmed the utterances with the Yoruba response "Ashe" to honor the interred Africans. Adding to the cultural complexity was Rev. Dr. James T. Yarsiah, an Episcopal minister. He asked the people to reflect on the meaning of the lives of those who went before, his lilting voice revealing his Liberian origins. Just before the final benediction, those assembled joined together in a chorus of "Precious Lord, Take My Hand."

In that moment the purpose of historic sites such as Drayton Hall became so clear. They allow us to connect with our past in the most poignant and visceral ways. When interpreted properly even the unlikely setting of a cemetery can be life-affirming. On that day in October, this one yielded new commitments to bury enmity and live life harmoniously. On that day a shared humanity was reaffirmed—even across the sometimes vast and bloody ground of race. Yes, Drayton Hall is much more than a house. ☽

Paris Mountain State Park, Greenville County. Courtesy of the South Caroliniana Library, University of South Carolina, Columbia.

Questing

Wandering solo,
nurturing soul with nature,
problems in pockets.

Deno Trakas

)

Lick Log Falls

I grew up at the foot of the Blue Ridge Mountains, in the town of Walhalla. But I never really knew them until I came back home. When I was a boy, "going up the mountain" meant time: seemingly endless Sunday rides up the sinuous switchbacks to places such as Long Creek and Mountain Rest, where my mother's side of the family lived. And though I was always happy to visit them—to run in my great-uncle's apple orchard or the dense woods behind his house—the trips felt like lifetimes: sleepy in the summer sun, my face against the vinyl seat of my father's convertible Bug. When I was ten, I made a single trip down the Chattooga River—a great "vein in the arm of God," as Ron Rash has put it. That day the river was flooded, well over four feet on the Highway 76 gauge, and my father and uncle were thrown from the raft. I floated a short distance alone, the raft wheeling as slowly as an autumn leaf. It was thrilling and terrifying and brief, and enough to confirm my single viewing of *Deliverance* as more documentary than imagination.

The better part of my childhood was spent either sitting in church or roaming in the woods, and when I left home at seventeen for the Citadel, it wasn't so much that I no longer wanted anything to do with either; more that both simply fell out of my life. When I finished the Citadel, I moved to Columbia, where I worked in a bookstore before entering graduate school at USC. My wife and I—we had gotten married just before our second year at Carolina—made frequent visits home, but we had no intention of returning. We had both left Walhalla with an equally resolute if hazy desire not to go back. But then Denise was offered a job as a speech-language therapist in Oconee County. I was completing my thesis, but that could be done from anywhere. We were students entering our mid-twenties; we were broke; she took the job, and we went home.

By good fortune my father had recently bought a small and long-unoccupied cabin on Lake Becky in Mountain Rest. We spent a week cleaning, painting, and refinishing the hardwood floors, and then we moved in. We got a dog, a beautiful yellow lab named Buddy, and while Denise drove down the mountain to work, I wrote in the mornings and in the afternoons began to explore. I found Lick Log Falls, and I found a small church.

It seems too convenient, too easy, to say that the long days Buddy and I began to spend in the woods corresponded to discovering Open Arms Tabernacle. But that doesn't make it any less true. What I had discarded had come back to me. Like T. S. Eliot I had returned, and in returning was knowing something—God, the forests—for the first time. It seems silly to say this happened to me in my mid-twenties. But it felt true then, and almost fifteen years later it feels true still. I would run the trails at Yellow Branch Falls or around the Oconee Fish Hatchery for hours while Buddy loped ahead of me, disappeared, and came barreling back. If I ran ten miles, then surely he ran twenty, diving in and out of creeks, his pink tongue dangling. I'm not certain the first time I heard of Lick Log Falls, but sometime that year we started going there, and for whatever reason we never stopped.

When I say Lick Log Falls, I am actually referring to the trails and area that descend wildly from a small trailhead at the end of two miles of dirt road down to Pig Pen Falls, on to Lick Log, and then down along the flat banks of the Chattooga. Over the years I've heard a number of explanations for the name: that the flat oval of clear land just beyond the pool of Pig Pen was once a literal pig pen; that Lick Log once marked an actual salt lick. But the land is steep and dense with white pines and mountain laurel and rhododendron. I can't imagine even the hardiest farmer penning his animals there. More likely, Pig Pen *looked* like a pig pen—you're struck by the flatness, the near-perfect symmetry of the natural clearing. Lick Log is impossibly steep, eighty feet long, and triple-tiered; but there is a way in a particular summer light that the falling water seems to lick the rocks and fallen trees, to curl back on itself in a clear, clean spray.

I thought about these things as Buddy and I ran up and down the trails. I thought of the novels I intended to write, the places I wanted to go; I thought of the things I intended to do and the things I already knew I wouldn't. I thought of Open Arms, the white clapboard church Denise

Lick Log Falls. Photograph by William M. Parker.

and I had started attending, small and obscure and alive with some power I had never before felt. Long after I finished my degree and was patching together teaching jobs at as many schools as would have me, I kept going to the falls four or five times a week. Many Sunday mornings Buddy and I would run early, dawn just beginning to gather and shape, and after that Denise and I would go to church and I would feel that I had simply exchanged holy for holy.

For years Denise and I came and went—Charleston, New Haven—but we always returned to the cabin, and I always returned to Lick Log. I came to feel possessive of it. Once, walking with Denise and Buddy, we passed a large group, loud and unruly with their voices and phones. It was evident to Denise how offended I was, and she gave me this look. *Would you rather they were at Walmart or some plastic place like Disneyland?* Well, no, I thought, but actually yes. Or if not there, at least not here. When I was teaching at Clemson in 2003, a student asked me for a good place he and his girlfriend might camp. I told him about Lick Log, and the following weekend saw him and his girlfriend packing their way out in the cool morning air. We stopped and talked, and I was delighted they had enjoyed the place. Then, maybe a month later, I ran in to find an entire fraternity camped along the trail, and something in me broke. In hindsight I see how important this ultimately was, this letting go, this shaving away of my false sense of possession. But at the time, I thought it would kill me.

This was *my* place, after all. I had spent the coldest night of my life camped with my brothers and friends down near the falls. Never—not living in the Northeast, nor in Eastern Europe, nor in the high mountains of Central Mexico—have I been colder. This is not empirically true, but in my mind, in my heart and skin and bones, I have never felt anything like that night the temperature fell into the low teens and the river skimmed with a foamy ice, while above us the stars swelled so fat and heavy they threatened to fall. Once, when my youngest brother was no more than eight, we hiked out in the pitch black of night—cold, soaked, and the battery in my headlamp dead. I took every friend who ever visited me there. It was the first place I took my son and daughter camping, my three-year-old daughter immediately stripping to her underwear and racing—to my panic—into the current. I ran—I must have run thousands of miles, thinking, praying. Angry, grateful, hungry. I knew this place at every time of day and night in every season. I had seen it in sun, rain, snow. This was *my* place.

But it isn't, not physically. And of course it never was. We moved away from Oconee County a long time ago. We sold the cabin. We buried Buddy. When I return now I am more likely to be walking with my wife and children than running alone. But the truth is, I don't return that often. The truth is, the area along the river has become over-camped, the sites barren of firewood, the trails worn just a little too deep. But that isn't the reason I seldom go back. There's a heaviness to returning. Where I once paid a physical price in my legs and lungs, what's asked of me now is emotional. The place is thick with memory, a repository of who I was, a way to understand who it is I have become and might yet be.

Besides, the river runs inside me now. The falls are internal, the topography an interior landscape. And in this way, finally, this really is my place. The soft loam of the trail, the way it gave beneath my feet; the rain-blown ferns so bright and dripping they appeared newly made. There is the day I was caught in a complete downpour and literally almost ran up on a wild sow and her piglets. There is Buddy, in and out of the river, wet as an otter, and smiling. There is the long climb back to the trailhead, and the moment you see the break in the foliage, the moment you see through the green to the blue of the sky and feel the air in your lungs and the blood in your body and the sweat on your face.

So much of me was made there; so much of me has never left. ☽

Margaret N. O'Shea

Peaceful Places

My favorite haven as a child was an apple tree with a just-so crook that formed my throne for pretending, my nest for hatching daydreams, and a hidden, quiet place to read or simply be. That was where I learned to be alone without being lonely—sometimes. Over the years, somewhere in time, I lost the need to climb a tree and lose myself in the boughs. I do still feel what I sensed as a child—that there is something important a tree will tell me if I listen.

The spiritual journey need not go far from home. I have been blessed with work in South Carolina that has taken me down memorable back roads with snippets of time to seek the peaceful places that define my sense of place and purpose. It is fine with me to be only one dot on a cosmic timeline. I like the places that remind me every dot is significant some-how, and without mine the continuum would be broken. In those special places, I feel connected to the past and the people I came from, and I feel closer to something greater than I am.

I have that feeling near a favorite tree that sprawls its gnarled branches out over the water from a bluff by the Cooper River in Moncks Corner. I believe it is a water oak, but names are not important in the relationship between me and the tree at Mepkin Abbey. I visit when I can. Especially in early morning and at dusk, when there is no commerce on the water, there is particular peace beneath the tree. The abbey is a community of Trappist monks, contemplative followers of the rule of Saint Benedict, including the principle of beginning again each day. That way of think-ing is important to me on a personal level, and I am at home with it. The brothers speak when necessary, but they pass most of their time in silence and prayer. If I am ever disturbed at Mepkin, it is by something I brought

The oak on the Cooper River, Mepkin Abbey. Photograph by Brandon Coffey.

with me down the long allée of oaks that line the entrance. I try to remember to lay down my burdens outside this holy place. Perhaps I can forget to pick them up again when I leave refreshed in a while.

My tree and the live oaks are ancients. The allée was shown on the earliest plats of the property when it was a colonial-era plantation owned by the Laurens family. Those oaks were present already around the time the city of Charleston was founded in 1671, and I suspect from its size and weathered look, my tree may be that old as well. The trees contribute to the sense of timelessness I value—I feel not so much that time is suspended at Mepkin but that time doesn't matter there except in the repetitive Liturgy of the Hours that mark it.

So I can sit and meditate on something or nothing.

The abbey was once a plantation later purchased by publisher Henry Luce and his ambassador wife, Clare Booth Luce. They donated the land to the Trappist monks in 1949. It measures three thousand acres, but the parts I have learned to know and love so far in my journey are the river bluff, the Luce and Laurens families' graves, formal gardens with roses and azaleas and a meadow of wildflowers. A primitive labyrinth lies east of the meadow. Another spiritual walk. Another meditation.

I have always figured I would not be a good nun, but I am good at wanting to be good. When I am at Mepkin Abbey, I try to spend some time with the carved wooden statues between the gardens and the bluff. They depict extremes in the life of Christ, one the Holy Family's flight into Egypt to keep the child safe from infanticide and the other his crucifixion. What draws me here goes beyond the art to the points of faith it invites me to ponder. I appreciate that towering oaks felled by Hurricane Hugo were lovingly carved into a new and different life form. And a different thought flits through my mind. The late Brother Lawrence had a nephew, David Drake, who had the artistry to achieve creation from destruction. Even the godly monks who know Somebody to help them in the life hereafter sometimes get by in this life by knowing somebody who knows somebody . . . at least that is how the statues came to be.

Part of what makes Mepkin Abbey special for me is the river so near the end of its passage to the sea. I love rivers. I have not gotten to know the Cooper River well, but I have spent some time on the rivers near where I live. Columbia is blessed to have three rivers, two of them breathtakingly scenic, especially when the Rocky Shoals spider lilies are in bloom. Sections of the Broad and Saluda seem deceptively far from a city, and those are my favorite parts. I like to let the paddles rest and just float a bit.

Some of my favorite views of the Saluda are from the woods by Riverbanks Zoo, where a half-mile trail runs from the botanical garden through the trees and past the ruins of an old water-powered textile mill, South Carolina's first. And some of the trails in Harbison State Forest provide spectacular glimpses of the Broad River.

What I love about rivers is that they start small and get all full of themselves until they become part of something bigger and grander. I think of mountain brooks upstate flowing over rocks as if chasing themselves and whistling like carefree boys with nothing else to do. But those waters flow into rivers, and the rivers flow into the ocean to hold great ships afloat. I am reminded that little boys must soon grow up from chasing dreams and whistling through their teeth to hold afloat perplexed and troubled worlds. My own familiar smaller scale is much the same. Calm water turns into rapids.

I like to look at water that stretches to the horizon, where lines of gray and coral meet, and imagine myself stretched out, so far, so wide, so deep, splashing only bits of what I am out on the face of the world. This too is my spiritual journey.

Johns Island Presbyterian Church. Photograph by Brandon Coffey.

Other places speak to me in ways that matter. I love the gray-whiskered canopy over Bohicket Road on Johns Island because it seems unspoiled. Such moss-shaded thoroughfares are not uncommon here, but only this one leads to what folks usually call simply "The Tree." Supposedly the oldest living thing east of the Rocky Mountains, the Angel Oak is said to be 1,500 years old. I don't know how one would go about proving or disproving the claim, but I believe it. For somebody like me who still believes trees have tales to tell, it's phenomenal to speculate what stories have fed this one. It stands more than 65 feet high and spreads 160 feet. Its trunk is 25 feet around. Where the Angel Oak stands is a public park now and less quiet than it used to be. Even so, it remains for me a place to pause and reflect.

Bohicket Road also takes me to the grounds around Johns Island Presbyterian Church, organized in 1710 and built in 1719. I read tombstones, and sometimes, driving someplace else or other, I pull over just to walk through cemeteries I can see from the road. They connect me to the past of a place and suggest fascinating stories about the people they honor. This particular cemetery contains something I've never seen anywhere else—a tall marble obelisk that marks the grave of a woman who died in 1855 and openly identifies her as the beloved "consort" of a local doctor, admitting for all to see what they were up to while she lived. It puts Hawthorne's puny little scarlet letter to shame, and I love it.

Another monument commemorates a wealthy planter's financial gifts. During his lifetime Thomas Hanscombe gave what today would be worth $1 million or more to the church, but he was buried in ignominy without a stone in the late 1880s because he had fathered several children with a mulatto woman. In 1910 the congregation erected a monument to recognize Hanscombe's generosity but, in a not-so-subtle gesture, turned its face away from the church.

Every old cemetery contains small reminders of how hard life was in the early years of this country. One of the most poignant is at Ebenezer United Methodist Church at Poole's Mill Crossroad near the Lexington-Orangeburg county line. The eight graves side by side are nineteenth-century resting places of a man and wife with their six little babies who all died in the first year of their lives. It was hard for little ones to survive in those times.

Ebenezer's is just one of the many church cemeteries that also contain the graves of Confederate soldiers who died nearby. The church is not far from Jeffcoat's Bridge, where Yankees stormed through in 1865 on their way to burn Columbia. The same sweep included the Battle of Aiken, and Union soldiers are buried alongside Rebels in downtown Aiken churchyards.

Columbia's Elmwood Cemetery has a Confederate section on the side nearest the point where the Broad and Saluda Rivers meet to form the Congaree. Even closer to the rivers is a potter's field and an area where unclaimed prisoners are buried.

Cemeteries draw me mainly because most of the dead have no one left to honor their presence in the world. Yet they all contributed something, known or not, popular or not in retrospect, to the world I live in today. So they are part of my journey too and my visits with them occasions of gratitude for those I have loved and lost and those who remain in my life.

What were those people and their families like? If we southerners do not attempt to understand ourselves, I think, we have no right to expect that of anyone else. Our past is so much more complex than it's made out to be, which is not to celebrate the worst but to acknowledge the good. So I am fascinated by small towns and farms where one does not visit without walking past the tombstones of a few dead ancestors. I know one family that has had soldiers in every war their country has fought since the American Revolution and Spanish-American War, and that's just since they came here from half a world away, where they also fought for what they perceived as freedom. Their hillside family cemetery is a monument to commitment that they are not about to disrespect.

An old man who had hunted all his life in the country woods around Branchville once showed me graves in the woods, the stones rubbed almost smooth, the 1700s dates barely legible. He told me he didn't know who was buried there, but he felt a connection and cleaned around the graves every now and then. He would continue doing that until he died. That's how I feel. Whether the stones are polished or faded, or whether the graves are marked with broken pottery and marbles as those of slaves and the poor used to be, we are connected somehow.

How to regard the past? I don't pretend to know for sure. It is a lot more complicated than simply avoiding some subjects in order to enjoy Thanksgiving dinner with family. I do know we can't change the past, but we have an opportunity in the present to shape the future. My own perspective has always been to look for ways we are all alike rather than focus on how we are different. It is one of the things I think about in the quiet places I love. ☽

Susan M. Boyer

A Little Something to
Take the Edge Off

Too many days, anxiety curls up in my core and hunkers down. I'm a card-carrying perfectionist, you see, with the associated gnawing need for every single thing I touch to be as perfect as my grandmother's lemon icebox pie.

I have my dream job. It's demanding, but I wouldn't trade it for Saturday night's Powerball jackpot. My sprawling family needs me to play my sundry roles—wife, mother, daughter, sister, cousin, aunt, niece, and —what the hell happened to my thirties?—grandmother. The sheer size of our clan renders it impossible for me to ever spend enough time with a single member. The ones I love most get me on a triage basis. Don't get me started on the laundry, the bills, or the errands. I juggle competing priorities while tap dancing on a giant rolling beach ball. I'm given to understand there's an epidemic of this frantically overcommitted stress syndrome, so I imagine you can relate. When I need a little something to take the edge off, I know exactly where I can get it.

I park on a side street and go in the back way—down behind the Governor's School in Greenville's West End. As soon as I cross the bridge over the creek and head down the hill, my tension subsides. Even in January, when most of the trees are bare, impudent patches of green greet me. Steel drum music wafts across from the Main Street entrance. A red awning winks at me from atop the hill across the lovingly landscaped grounds. I reach the top of the steps that will take me down into Falls Park and draw a deep, slow breath.

Couples sprawl on picnic blankets on the grass. A golden retriever strains on his leash as he greets a mixed breed who's equally happy to see

Sunday in the park. Photograph by James Boyer.

a friend. Tweens climb on the very river rocks the signs warn them off. A blue Frisbee flies across my line of sight. On swings, benches, and quilts, folks are lost in books. A ding alerts me that bicyclists are passing behind me. In groups, pairs and alone, folks wander the park paths.

I let myself be folded into the vignette before me. It's as though I've joined something that's one part party, one part carnival. And though I don't know a single person, I'm immediately at ease. I've arrived, and by showing up have become part of the scene playing out. There's an unspoken sense of camaraderie in that we're all there for the same thing: to soak up the extravagant beauty of a Sunday afternoon, to drink it in and be filled.

Someone has already taken my favorite place on the swing with the best view of the falls, but no matter. I perch on the stacked-stone wall and soak in the harmony of the Reedy River rushing over rocks and the music of steel drums. Another day it might have been guitar music, or saxophone. In the background, muted, is another kind of music, that of happy children playing, and snippets of conversations as kindred spirits pass by.

The Liberty Bridge curves against the backdrop of a crystal-clear Carolina blue sky, suspended through the treetops high enough above the falls not to obscure the view. I watch white water spilling over sheets of rock and boulders in multiple spots, each section of the falls with its own grace and pitch. The water congregates in the pool below. Ducks glide across the surface.

The swaths of grass and walkways are bordered by meticulously tended beds. Some plants are dormant, others blooming, still others bursting from the ground in an astonishing array of greens. I'm not a gardener, so I can't call the shrubs, flowers, vines, or ferns by name. But I can revel in the lushness, especially in January. In May this garden will rival all others, the blooms stunning in their flamboyant reds, yellows, purples, blues, and pinks.

After a while I meander farther down the path, take another flight of rock steps down toward the river. In a moment I'm standing on a rolling plateau of granite, or maybe it's limestone. Unlike the stacked-stone walls and bed borders, these rocks were likely here when the Cherokee used Greenville as a hunting ground. I watch the water as the mystified ghosts of others who stood where I now stand puzzle over the man-wrought changes to the riverfront and the tableau—both animated and tranquil—surrounding it.

A thirty-something couple shares a private smile and vacates a swing to my right, and I take their place. He places his hand on the small of her back and murmurs something to her as they climb the steps. Warmth and a promise radiate from her uplifted face.

I turn back to the water and push my feet against the slate pad to rock the swing. Back and forth, back and forth. My breathing synchronizes with the rhythm. I can no longer hear the music. The quiet settles around me. I rock until the shade here chills me.

When I head back up to the wide expanse of park, I've stepped from a private room back into the party. The simultaneous buzz of activity and peace enfold me. All around me people are smiling, laughing. I cross the bridge over the creek, returning smiles to everyone I pass. To my left the raised circle of grass bordered by stone speaks to me of lazy summer afternoons with Shakespeare in the park.

Behind a toddler grasping his mother's hand, I make my way to the steps and begin the climb. Halfway up, she apologizes for the pace.

"No hurry," I tell her.

On the plaza at the top of the park, near the entrance to the Liberty Bridge, I pause for a moment at the spot where a young groom-to-be staged a flash mob dance proposal to the tune of Bruno Mars's "Marry

You" back in September. A few years back, another suitor spelled out "Will You Marry Me" in candles on one of the overlook platforms on Christmas Eve. My eyes moisten. Romance thrives in this magical place.

Another flight of steps and moments later, I'm standing by the fountain that marks the Main Street entrance to the park. Savory aromas from nearby restaurants tempt me to linger a while at a table for one with a glass of wine and a bowl of something warm.

But I have what I came for. I am not only calm, but a quiet joy has displaced the anxiety. I turn left on Main Street and circle back to my car. ☽

Alex Sanders

)

The Magic of Mepkin

Mepkin Abbey is a Trappist monastery located at the junction of two forks of the Cooper River, northwest of Charleston in Berkeley County, South Carolina. The name is from the Cusabo Indians, who called the area Makkean. Mepkin Plantation was the estate of several historic families. In 1681 the property was granted to the sons of Sir John Colleton, one of South Carolina's Lords Proprietor. In 1762 Landgrave John Colleton sold the property to the early American patriot Henry Laurens. Mepkin became his main place of residence.

Shortly thereafter Laurens became the first president of the Continental Congress. He was captured by the British during the American Revolution. British soldiers burned his home at Mepkin to the ground. He was released for Lord Cornwallis in a prisoner exchange. He signed the 1783 Treaty of Paris for the new nation, formally ending the American Revolution. His ashes are buried at Mepkin in a picturesque cemetery overlooking the Cooper River.

After the Civil War, Mepkin, like other South Carolina plantations, fell into the hands of wealthy northerners. In 1936 the property was acquired by Henry Luce, publisher of *Time, Life,* and *Fortune* magazines. He was married to the glamorous congresswoman, ambassador, and playwright Clare Boothe Luce. They made Mepkin their home. Luce was recognized as the most influential private citizen of his day. He was deeply religious his whole life, having been born in Dengzhou, China, the child of Christian missionaries. At his direction Pope John Paul II was pictured on the cover of *Time* magazine on fifteen separate occasions. The Virgin Mary appeared ten times. Billy Graham's career took off after Luce traveled to nearby

Columbia to attend one of his early crusades. He was much taken with the young evangelist and put his picture on the cover of *Life* magazine.

In 1949 Luce and his wife donated a large portion of Mepkin for the founding of a monastic community. Mepkin Abbey was established there the same year as a Trappist monastery. Luce's ashes are buried on the grounds of the monastery with those of Henry Laurens.

I had vaguely heard of the magical qualities of Mepkin. I dismissed the idea as superstition until I quite unexpectedly experienced the magic first-hand. In election year 2002, I was the Democratic nominee from South Carolina to succeed the legendary J. Strom Thurmond (R-SC). The venture was quixotic at best. As every schoolchild knows, the states are divided for political purposes into two groups. The red states are the Republican states and the blue states the Democratic states. South Carolina is easily the reddest of the red states—redder than red, crimson, fuchsia, magenta, a color all its own. Unsurprisingly I lost.

Soon after losing the election, I trudged burro-like back home to Charleston. With me was Zoe, my wife of fifty years, and our two surrogate children, a small gray kitten named Maggie Pennington and Neil Diamond, a ten-year-old canary. Within days of our arrival, little Maggie escaped and was run over by a car. Her short life ended in Zoe's arms. The next day Neil Diamond fell from his perch like a stone and expired without a chirp.

I was rapidly closing in on my biblically allotted three score years and ten. For all practical purposes, I was broke, unemployed, and homeless. I was enveloped with the dread of becoming uninspired. Near the end of the campaign, Zoe had said that if I lost the election, I would have to move to some other state. I couldn't help but notice she had said *I* would have to move, not *we* would have to move. Who would ever have imagined I would find redemption in a Trappist monastery?

Dispirited and despairing, I awoke early one morning after we arrived in Charleston on the second floor of the diminutive carriage house we were temporarily renting. (In less elegant environs than Charleston, carriage houses are called garage apartments.) The weather matched my melancholy. Unseasonable frigid temperatures gripped Charleston. A freezing rain was falling. I stumbled outside in my pajamas, found a nearby vending machine, and bought a copy of the *Post and Courier,* the local newspaper that had endorsed my opponent in the election. In fact I got two copies of the newspaper, one for me and one for Zoe. I find, when buying newspapers from vending machines, you can get multiple copies for the

Mepkin Abbey gates. Photograph by Brandon Coffey.

price of a single copy. No point, I thought, in maximizing the profits of a publication that had so enthusiastically supported my opponent.*

That particular morning the *Post and Courier* carried a mildly interesting feature story about Mepkin Abbey. According to the story, the monks of Mepkin had temporarily detoured from their lives of solitude to undertake an uncharacteristically worldly endeavor. They were making fruitcakes. One of their number had been designated to meet visitors at the gates of the monastery and converse sufficiently to sell the fruitcakes for the modest sum of eight dollars each. I immediately sprang from my lethargy, determined to find Mepkin Abbey and buy a fruitcake. I had never much liked fruitcake. Actually I'd always hated fruitcake. It's one of the few Christmas gifts I never could bring myself to regift. But now I had a purpose in life. Perhaps that's a little overstated. At the least, for the first time since the election, I had something to do besides feel sorry for myself.

I departed on my doubtful pilgrimage, driving endlessly through the bowels of the South Carolina lowcountry, stopping at every country store

---

*Note to the newspaper police: I really didn't steal a fifty-cent newspaper. That's a joke. If I wanted to take retribution against the *Post and Courier*, I would do something considerably worse than that.

Man and miracle. Photograph by Patti Goff.

and crossroads to ask directions and trying hard to forget election year 2002. My progress was substantially impeded by the terribly inclement weather. Clouds hung oppressively low in the heavens. The freezing rain continued unabated. Fog shrouded the swampy landscape. The tangled branches of towering live oak trees on either side of the road wove themselves together to form tunnels for me to pass through. At last the brick gates of Mepkin Abbey loomed before me. Edgar Allan Poe's House of Usher was never more imposing. Or should I say spooky?

Just as the *Post and Courier* had reported, the designated monk was waiting for me, as if he had been anticipating my arrival his whole life. Perhaps he had been. He was dressed in the traditional habit of a monk, a simply constructed garment of rough brown sackcloth, with a floppy hood and a rope sash tied loosely at the waist. I imagined him to have once been a titan of business or industry or, perhaps, one of the masters of the universe described by Tom Wolfe in *Bonfire of the Vanities,* now determined to repent and forsake the world and all its mortal pleasures.

I could scarcely see his face. His eyes seemed to glow like smoldering embers in the scant illumination beneath his hood. (Maybe that was my imagination.) I got out of my car and handed him a five dollar bill and three singles. Silently he handed me back a fruitcake, wrapped in brown paper. I did not speak. Nor did he. Somehow small talk seemed inappropriate. Then, just as I was about to leave, he leaned so close to me that I could feel his warm breath on my cold face. He spoke.

"We all voted for you," he said.

"I'm amazed," I stammered. "I had no idea y'all voted."

"Oh yes, we always vote," he said, "and we voted for you."

"That makes me think God is a Democrat," I said.

He leaned even closer and whispered in my ear, "God *is* a Democrat."

At that very instant, the rain stopped, the skies opened, and the sun shone forth. I drove back to Charleston, the redeeming words of the talkative monk ringing in my ears, his fruitcake on the seat beside me. Then Johnny Nash's timeless lyrics came on the car radio: "Gone are the dark clouds that had me blind / It's gonna be a bright, bright sunshiny day."

Mepkin had worked its magic. As Billy Graham might say, I was born again. I even began to like fruitcake. ☽

"In the world to come, it will always be morning." Photograph by Larry Cameron.

Morning, Reprise

Heaven

In the world to come, it will always be
morning, somewhere between breakfast cooking
and snow, and still time to stretch against clean
sheets, clean every night, our bed made ever new,
love reaching back, the children angels but well,
asleep in another room, their own dreams.
Outside, the wind will blow peach-blossom petals.
We will know everything and forget it.
The house will be paid for and all our needs,
yet thirst and desire will keep a place: wars
no more, though reasonable argument; words
will fail but kisses complete, the spring eternal
with weather, storms, solstices every day
and summer still to urge the garden. Then will be now,
tomorrow closer, today farther away.
God will reveal himself a soft, speechless hand
to hold us, rub us, as he would love
from looking-glass or greed from gold.
He won't blame us for our cross beginnings,
or remind us of the end, put off now forever.

All will be sky, clear and weightless and blue.
It is so wonderful I could go on.
But first we must turn away, wink at the dust
that catches in the corner, fills our breaths,
and cry for the beauty we cannot explain,
so pale and purposeless we are told, so rich
we know, so much like the spotless world to come.

Starkey Flythe Jr. (1935–2013), from *Paying the Anesthesiologist*, 1995

)

Afterword

The Same, yet Different

It's a moment I've come to expect. I'm at an event in Beaufort or Charleston, Columbia or maybe Greenville, and I'm introduced to someone, a new acquaintance. A knowing look, a tilt of the head, and the inevitable nod of understanding. Then the question, which usually takes one of two forms. "You're not from here, are you?" Or, "Where are you from— originally, I mean?"

That question, and I'm busted. And no, it's not because I'm a Yankee. I've lived in South Carolina for the past nineteen years, and in the South my entire life. I have never, ever been mistaken for a Brit, a Canadian, Australian, or New Zealander, no matter where I've traveled. Just doesn't happen. I am cursed (or blessed, depending on one's point of view) with the most appalling southern accent imaginable. True, I was born and raised in LA, but that's what the locals call Lower Alabama. I'm from the heart of *Dixie,* for God's sake. I speak, and I sound like I'm wading through grits while eating corn pone dripping with molasses. But as a native son or daughter of South Carolina can tell immediately—soon as I open my mouth—I'm not *from* here. We might all be southerners in these parts, but we sound different.

Except for two-plus years in Atlanta in the seventies (which really doesn't count, since Hotlanta is the New York City of the South), I've never lived anywhere except Alabama and Beaufort County, South Carolina. When I moved here almost two decades ago, I didn't expect South Carolina to be any different. I certainly didn't expect folks here to sound different. After all, growing up I'd spent a lot of time in Georgia and

Mississippi and especially in Florida, my mother's home state. No one there ever asked me where I was from. We talked alike. We spoke fluent cracker, and we understood each other. We ate the same food, drank the same brew, and had the same expressions: we were always fixing to do stuff; up and quitting someone; yelling shit-fire-and-save-matches; having a bait of that; not knowing pea-turkey squat or having the sense God promised a billy goat.

There were a few amusing diversions in our sameness, however. In the southeast corner of Alabama where I grew up, peanuts ruled. My father was a peanut farmer, as were most of my relatives and everybody else I knew. My grandfather is credited with being the first commercial peanut farmer in the Southeast. After meeting George Washington Carver, my grandfather and his brother risked everything to buy a newfangled peanut harvester, the first one anyone in the area had ever seen. Until then peanuts were lifted from the ground with a pitchfork and fed to the hogs. When I was growing up, one of the most exciting social events in rural life was the peanut boil. In the closest town to our farm, there was a peanut festival and parade, where a peanut queen was crowned. There was even a Little Miss Peanut. When I went north to college (a few miles outside of Birmingham), my new friends howled with laughter when I told them about one of my high school hangouts, the Goober Drive-in. Their laughter made no sense to me; back home we often called each other goobers, which was a term of endearment, even though it sort of meant country bumpkin. But I learned quickly that up north, "goober" had a different meaning.

Since I've been in South Carolina, I've seen goobers of all kinds. But here, they're not peanuts, and I dare not call anyone a goober, even fondly. Back in Alabama my grandfather's pride and joy, in addition to the goobers, was a precisely rowed pecan orchard, in a long, fenced-off field next to the house. Every fall my sisters and I earned money to buy Christmas presents by picking up pecans and selling them. Mostly, though, we ate them and cooked with them. Pecans were as much a part of my raising as peanuts and a major food source. Let me put it this way: my grandfather had a pe-con orchard, and we picked up pe-cons for Christmas money. We ate them all year long. We toasted pe-cons, made pe-con pies, and filled brownies, fudge, and fruitcakes with them. In South Carolina I do the same. But here I do it with pee-*can*s.

Then there's the long *i*. Where I came from, an *i* is very much like the sound you make when the doctor orders you to open wide and inserts a tongue depressor, except that it's a little higher-pitched. Ask me to say "nice white rice," and then ask a native South Carolinian. Even in Charleston, where they grow the stuff, he or she will say in a honeyed, French Huguenot–based drawl, "Nice. White. Rice." I will say "Nii-ah-ce wh-ii-aht ri-aah-ce," the way we say it in LA. When I ask for ice in South Carolina, even in Bubba's filling station thirteen miles from nowhere, I'm likely to get a puzzled look. "What you need, young lady?" Ah-esse, I'll say, but the more I enunciate, the worse it gets. I practice at home, before going to a party. "White wine would be nice, thank you," I'll say crisply, hoping to sound like the Queen Mother. My host is more likely to understand me, I've discovered, if I say it faster and clip off the words. My normal speech pattern is a throwback to the days of vinyl: a forty-five played at thirty-three-and-a-third.

With my south Alabama drawl, extra syllables tend to appear where none existed before. As a consequence even my husband and my in-laws, all of whom have lived most of their lives in South Carolina and either are, or consider themselves to be, natives, have trouble communicating with their Alabama sister-in-law. Last summer, when the grandkids were here at the beach house on Fripp Island, I announced that Jim, my brother-in-law, would be arriving in time for dinner.

The family: "I thought Jean and Mike were coming tomorrow."

Me: "Not Jean—*Jim*. Gee-ah-mm."

My husband's hearing loss adds to the confusion. Later that day I'm telling him the reason we're pulling the golf cart out.

Me: "Molly and I are going to the beach. We want to try out the new kayak."

My husband, looking up at the sky: "It's not very windy today."

Me, in exasperation: "Not the kite, the kayak. Ki-*yak*. *YAK*!"

My husband: "Jack? I thought you said Molly was going."

It's not just my Southern accent that's different. South Carolina food is the same as the food I grew up with, but with distinct variations. Except on hamburger buns and Chinese food, I rarely saw or consumed sesame seeds until moving to the lowcountry. Around here people eat them in thin, sweet wafers, and I thought for a long time that benne and sesame seeds looked suspiciously alike. "Sesame cookies, right?" I asked a Charlestonian, who served them on a silver platter. Her horrified response was "Oh, no, sugar—in Charleston, we only use benne seeds."

The first barbecue I attended in South Carolina was an eye-opener. Granted, there are a few joints in Birmingham that serve an unusual, mayo-based sauce (known, appropriately, as Alabama white sauce), but

Battery Creek. Photograph courtesy of the author.

otherwise barbecue sauce is red. Might be thin and vinegary or thick and
syrupy, but you can count on it being *red*. In Beaufort I was handed my
first plate of South Carolina barbecue, hot off the grill. Everybody else was
eating theirs with great relish, apparently not noticing—or caring—that
it had gone bad and turned yellow. I was about to fall back on my usual
excuse when served a steak or other red meat, that I'm a recovering vegetarian, when I spotted the real barbecue in a big pot. More brown than
red, and sort of soupy-looking, but at least it wasn't yellow. With relief I
grabbed the serving spoon and was about to put it on a hamburger bun
when the host stopped me. Hold on, he said, as he practically covered
my plate with rice. Then, to my astonishment, he spooned the barbecue
over it. Must be a South Carolina thing, I thought as I took a tentative
bite. Back home, we eat bread with our barbecue; here, they grow and eat
rice. It was delicious, and I gobbled it up, but after a few bites I'd made a
discovery: what I was eating wasn't barbecue after all, but a kissing cousin
of Brunswick stew, which we always had with barbecue when I was growing up. It was served in bowls, though, never with rice. Here they call it
hash.

Seafood is another thing as well. Because I was raised a few miles from the Florida line, seafood was a staple of our diet. During oyster season my father would sometimes let me come along on his weekly runs to Apalachicola for their famous oysters. He bought them by the bushel, in fat rough clusters, always getting enough to share with relatives and neighbors. Daddy prided himself on being such a fast oyster-shucker that he could have one ready and sitting in front of you by the time you doused yours with hot sauce and tipped it down your throat. His method was not for me, though. My husband rolls his eyes at the way I eat raw oysters. Right out of the shell and down the gullet was considered unladylike for southern belles of my day. I still eat them the way my mother, sisters, and all the females I knew did, by putting one on a cracker, dabbing it with cocktail sauce, and stuffing the whole thing in. You have to be careful to select a small oyster, however, or you'll end up looking like a rather unladylike chipmunk.

My husband was introduced to my family, his new Alabama relatives, with the ritual of the Apalachicola oyster run. Because of that initiation, he was surprised to find out that I'd never attended an oyster roast until I moved to South Carolina. ("Have you ever been to a peanut boil?" I countered.) Oysters on the half shell were as much a part of our Christmas visits to LA as fruit cake, and oyster stew was traditional Christmas Eve fare in the King household. But oyster roasts? It was a freezing cold but bright blue day when I attended my first one here, on the lawn of a splendid plantation somewhere near Johns Island. Charleston's *Garden & Gun* magazine was not born then, but if it had been, this occasion would've been the perfect full-page spread. Everywhere I looked there were beautiful, golden-hued people dressed in hunting jackets, with cashmere scarves and high leather boots. Several feet away from the burlap-steamed oyster pit was a long, rustic table, laden with incredibly delicious dishes, from gratins and fancy salads to a wide selection of gourmet desserts. But the oysters! I almost made myself sick eating so many, and I came away thinking there's no finer way to prepare them. As disloyal as it sounds, I'll take a South Carolina oyster roast over an Alabama peanut boil any day.

The thing is, after nineteen years, I have become a South Carolinian, in my heart and soul. You might still have to ask me to repeat myself when I request more ice, another serving of rice, or a nice glass of white wine. When I introduce myself to you, tell me to speak faster, not louder, and you'll probably catch my name the first time, without all the superfluous syllables. Come to see us in Beaufort, and I might serve you pe-con pie or boiled peanuts or tea without enough sugar in it to put you in a diabetic coma (I only *thought* I'd had sweet tea until I moved here), but you'll know that my heart is in the right place. I'm where I should be. Here is where my ashes will be scattered one day, into the gentle ebb and flow of Battery Creek, which I look at every day. Every blessed day, in Beaufort, South Carolina. ☽

CONTRIBUTORS

PILLEY BIANCHI (aka Deb Pilley) is the youngest daughter of John and Sally Pilley. She has most recently collaborated with her father and his co-author Hilary Hinzmann on *Chaser, Unlocking the Genius of the Dog Who Knows 1000 Words* and is teaming with them again on their new book along with her sister Robin. Bianchi lives with her family in Brooklyn, New York, where she is an award-winning songwriter, pianist and composer. After an extensive career in the entertainment industry, she never imagined her greatest and most rewarding success would revolve around an old man and his dog.

KIM BOYKIN's books are well reviewed and, according to RT Book Reviews, feel like they're being told across a kitchen table. She is the author of *A Peach of a Pair, Palmetto Moon,* and *The Wisdom of Hair* from Penguin Random House's Berkley Books, and *Echoes of Mercy* from River's Edge Media. While her heart is always in South Carolina, she lives in Charlotte and has a heart for hairstylists, librarians, and book junkies like herself. Find her at www.KimBoykin.com.

SUSAN M. BOYER is the author of the *USA Today* bestselling Liz Talbot mystery series. Her debut novel, *Lowcountry Boil,* won the 2012 Agatha Award for best first novel. Her short fiction has appeared in *moonShine review, Spinetingler Magazine,* and *Relief Journal,* among others. Originally from Faith, North Carolina, Boyer lives in Greenville, South Carolina, with her husband. They spend a considerable amount of time hanging out along the South Carolina coast. Learn more at www.susanmboyer.com.

Past president of the Southern Historical Association, ORVILLE VERNON BURTON is Creativity Professor of Humanities, professor of history, sociology, and computer science at Clemson University, and director of the Clemson CyberInstitute. From 2008–2010 he was the Burroughs Distinguished Professor of Southern

History and Culture at Coastal Carolina University. He is emeritus University Distinguished Teacher/Scholar, University Scholar, and professor of history, African American studies, Pan African Studies, and sociology at the University of Illinois. Burton is the author of more than two hundred articles and author or editor of more than twenty books, including *The Age of Lincoln, In My Father's House Are Many Mansions: Family and Community in Edgefield, South Carolina, Penn Center: A History Preserved.* Among his honors are fellowships and grants from the Rockefeller Foundation, the National Endowment for the Humanities, the Pew Foundation, the National Science Foundation, the American Council of Learned Societies, the Woodrow Wilson International Center for Scholars, the National Humanities Center, the US Department of Education, National Park Service, and the Carnegie Foundation. In 2017 he received the Governor's Award in the Humanities

EMILY CLAY lives in Columbia and is publisher of *Columbia Metropolitan* magazine, which she started with her husband in 1990. She grew up on the coast and spent many years crabbing, fishing, and shrimping with her beloved grandmother, Mary Ravenel Gignilliat. It has been her great joy to watch her daughters, Mary, Helen, and Margaret, embrace her grandmother's lifelong love affair with the salt water.

MARIAN WRIGHT EDELMAN, founder and president of the Children's Defense Fund, has been an advocate for disadvantaged Americans for her entire professional life. A Bennettsville native and graduate of Spelman College and Yale Law School, Edelman was the first black woman admitted to the Mississippi Bar and directed the NAACP Legal Defense and Educational Fund office in Jackson, Mississippi. She has received more than one hundred honorary degrees and many awards, including the Albert Schweitzer Humanitarian Prize, the Heinz Award, a MacArthur Foundation Prize Fellowship, the Presidential Medal of Freedom (the nation's highest civilian award), and the Robert F. Kennedy Lifetime Achievement Award for her writings, which include *Families in Peril: An Agenda for Social Change; The Measure of Our Success: A Letter to My Children and Yours; Lanterns: A Memoir of Mentors; I'm Your Child, God: Prayers for Our Children; I Can Make a Difference: A Treasury to Inspire Our Children;* and *The Sea Is So Wide and My Boat Is So Small: Charting a Course for the Next Generation.* She is married to Peter Edelman, a professor at Georgetown University Law Center. They have three sons and four grandchildren.

Historian and public radio host WALTER EDGAR retired from the University of South Carolina after teaching for forty years. He is the author of *South Carolina: A History* and *Partisans and Redcoats: The Southern Conflict That Turned the Tide of the American Revolution* and was the editor for *The South Carolina Encyclopedia.*

For a number of years, he has grown heritage camellias. Since retiring he has gone back to growing annuals from seed—just as his grandfather taught him to do.

NIKKY FINNEY was born by the sea in South Carolina and raised during the civil rights, Black Power, and Black Arts movements. She began reading and writing poetry as a teenager growing up in the spectacle and human theater of the Deep South. At Talladega College she began to explore autodidactically the great intersections between art, history, politics, and culture. These same arenas of exploration are ongoing today in her writing, teaching, and spirited belief in one-on-one activism. She is the author of four books of poetry, *On Wings Made of Gauze, RICE, The World Is Round,* and *Head Off & Split,* which won the National Book Award for Poetry in 2011. For twenty-one years she taught creative writing at the University of Kentucky and now holds the John H. Bennett, Jr., Chair in Creative Writing and Southern Letters at the University of South Carolina in Columbia.

MINDY FRIDDLE is the author of novels *The Garden Angel,* selected for Barnes and Noble's Discover Great New Writers program, and *Secret Keepers,* winner of the Willie Morris Award for Southern Fiction. The SC Arts Commission granted her a fellowship in prose and she has twice won the South Carolina Fiction Prize. Her short stories have appeared in *Hayden's Ferry Review, Southern Humanities Review, Phoebe, Steel Toe Review, A Long Story,* and *Litmag.* Friddle earned her MFA in fiction from Warren Wilson College. She lives in Greenville.

KENDRA HAMILTON's poetry has appeared in *Callaloo,* the *Southern Review, Shenandoah,* and anthologies including *Angles of Ascent: A Norton Anthology of Contemporary African American Poetry, Black Nature: Four Centuries of African American Nature Poetry,* and *Shaping Memories: Reflections of 25 African American Women Writers.* A member of the Cave Canem and Wintergreen Women writer's collectives, she is a faculty member at Presbyterian College in Clinton, South Carolina, and the author of *The Goddess of Gumbo* and *Romancing the Gullah,* a book of literary criticism.

KRISTINE HARTVIGSEN is a Greenville-based writer who works in nonprofit communications. She began her career at the *State* and the *Columbia Record* newspapers and is a contributor and past associate editor of *Jasper Magazine.* She also is a past editor of *South Carolina Business, Lake Murray–Columbia,* and *Columbia Northeast* magazines, as well as a past contributing editor of *undefined* magazine. Hartvigsen was a finalist in the South Carolina Poetry Initiative's Single Poem Contest in 2010 and 2011. In 2012 Muddy Ford Press published her poetry chapbook, *To the Wren Nesting.* She doesn't play softball regularly anymore but has held on to her equipment and is game should an invitation be in the offing. She is the proud mom of a US soldier and two rescue dogs.

New York Times bestselling author **PATTI CALLAHAN HENRY** has published eleven novels: *Losing the Moon, Where the River Runs, When Light Breaks, Between the Tides, The Art of Keeping Secrets, Driftwood Summer, The Perfect Love Song, Coming up for Air, And Then I Found You, The Stories We Tell,* and *The Idea of Love.* Her twelfth novel, *The Bookshop at Water's End,* was released in June 2017. On October 9, 2018, her novel *The Consolation of Joy: The Improbable Love Story of C. S. Lewis and Joy Davidman* will be released. Hailed as a fresh new voice in southern fiction, Henry has been shortlisted for the Townsend Prize for Fiction and nominated numerous times for the Southeastern Independent Booksellers Novel of the Year. Her work is published in five languages, and all novels can be found on audio. She lives in Mountain Brook, Alabama, and Bluffton, South Carolina.

After a few years as a newspaper and TV reporter, Blythewood resident **CHRIS HORN** began a writing career at his alma mater, the University of South Carolina. Over the years he has contributed to two books about USC: *University of South Carolina: A Portrait* and *A Spirit of Place.* When he's not busy writing or podcasting, he's often on the water, in search of the elusive "lunker mouth" bass.

JOHN JAKES sold his first story (science fiction, 1,500 words) when he was eighteen and has written professionally ever since. He continued to write and sell books, short stories, and plays during a sojourn in advertising that lasted seventeen years. Then, in 1971, he began to write full time, gaining worldwide success with historical novels. His many appearances on the *New York Times* bestseller list include several volumes of *The Kent Family Chronicles* and all three novels of the *North and South* trilogy. Jakes and his wife, Rachel, lived in South Carolina for thirty-two years before moving to Florida.

CASSANDRA KING is the *New York Times* bestselling author of five novels and a book of nonfiction as well as numerous stories, articles, and essays. She was raised on a peanut farm in LA (lower Alabama) that has been in the King family for generations. Currently she's working on a memoir/cookbook about life with her late husband, Pat Conroy.

DAVID LAUDERDALE is a senior editor at the *Island Packet* and *Beaufort Gazette* daily newspapers, where he writes columns and editorials about lowcountry life. He has been in the *Packet* newsroom for the most part since 1977, having also worked as a reporter, managing editor, and editorial page editor. His writing has won many state and regional honors. Recognized for coverage of Gullah culture, the environment, mental health, literacy, and local history, Lauderdale is a popular public speaker. He teaches an adult Sunday school class called "Lowcountry Lessons" at First Presbyterian Church on Hilton Head Island, where he lives.

Siblings **MATT LEE** and **TED LEE** grew up and learned to cook in Charleston in a townhouse on the city's fabled Rainbow Row. When they left to attend colleges in the Northeast, they so missed the foods of their hometown that they founded *The Lee Bros. Boiled Peanuts Catalogue,* a mail-order catalog for southern pantry staples and, of course, boiled peanuts. When an editor of a travel magazine asked them to write a story about road-tripping their home state in search of great food, they embarked on a second career as food journalists and cookbook authors. Since 2000 they have written hundreds of food, wine, and travel features for magazines and newspapers, including the *New York Times, Travel + Leisure, Martha Stewart Living, Southern Living, Saveur, Bon Appétit,* and *Food & Wine.* Their three cookbooks, *The Lee Bros. Southern Cookbook* (2007), *The Lee Bros. Simple Fresh Southern* (2009), and *The Lee Bros. Charleston Kitchen* (2013), have, combined, won six James Beard and IACP Awards, and they are widely credited with bringing a richer understanding of southern cooking into the mainstream. They were on-air commentators for all seven seasons of the Cooking Channel's hit series *Unique Eats,* and they currently are the stars and executive producers of *Southern Uncovered with The Lee Bros.* on Ovation. Matt, his wife, Gia, and their three sons live in Charleston. Ted lives with his wife, the artist E. V. Day, in Brooklyn, New York.

MELINDA LONG is the author of several children's books, including *How I Became a Pirate, Pirates Don't Change Diapers,* and *The Twelve Days of Christmas in South Carolina.* Her pirate books have also been adapted for the stage. She is the mother of two adult kids, Cathy and Bryan, and has been married to Thom, her husband, since 1984. Melinda thinks he's a keeper even if he doesn't like peanut butter pie.

New York Times and *USA Today* bestselling author of more than forty novels, former pediatric ER doctor **CJ LYONS** has lived the life she writes about in her Thrillers with Heart. Her novels have twice won the International Thriller Writers' prestigious Thriller Award, the RT Reviewers' Choice Award, the Readers' Choice Award, the RT Seal of Excellence, and the Daphne du Maurier Award for Excellence in Mystery and Suspense. She lives on Hilton Head Island. Learn more at www.CJLyons.net.

TOM MACK began his career as a member of the English Department at the University of South Carolina–Aiken in 1976. He now holds the rank of Distinguished Professor Emeritus. He has published to date more than one hundred articles on American literature and cultural history and five books, including *Circling the Savannah, Hidden History of Aiken County, Hidden History of Augusta, A Shared Voice,* and *The South Carolina Encyclopedia Guide to South Carolina Writers.* Since 1990 Mack has also contributed a weekly column to the *Aiken Standard*—more than 1,400 columns to date devoted to the arts and humanities. In recognition of his work as a cultural critic, he received the 2013 Media Arts Award from the Greater Augusta Arts Council. Mack has also served as chair of the board of governors of the South Carolina Academy of Authors, the organization responsible for managing the state's literary hall of fame. Mack currently serves as vice chair of the board of South Carolina Humanities and as a member of the advisory council of the Etherredge Center for the Performing Arts. For his many contributions to the cultural life of Aiken and South Carolina, Mack was presented with the Governor's Award in the Humanities in 2014.

MICHAEL L. MILLER is a retired journalist living in Columbia. He's the author of two books, a biography of the rock band Hootie & the Blowfish and a collection of short stories, *Lonesome Pines*. He's also retired from surfing but still enjoys swimming laps in the pool and taking the occasional dip in the ocean. A few years ago, he donated his last surfboard to the next-door neighbors' daughters, who were seven and eight at the time. Now they're twelve and thirteen, living at Folly Beach, surfing every chance they get, and even competing in surfing contests. This makes him very happy.

MARGARET N. O'SHEA is a writer and editor whose thirty-eight years as a journalist were spent writing mainly about South Carolina's people, the places they live and work, and the issues that affect their lives. She was sixteen when her first 1-A story appeared in the *Columbia Record,* where she worked while attending college, beginning a lifelong dedication to the craft and the state where she chose to practice it. After a stint at the *Southern Illinoisan* in Carbondale while in graduate school, she came home and for nearly three decades wrote for the *State* and the South Carolina bureau of the *Augusta Chronicle,* receiving more than 150 state, local, and national awards for her work. O'Shea is author of ninety-eight children's stories that originally appeared in the *State Magazine,* and her articles also have appeared in *Newsweek,* the *Chicago Tribune,* the *St. Louis Post-Dispatch, Notre Dame Magazine,* and *National Catholic Reporter.* Since 2001 most of her writing has been for a limited audience as a mitigation specialist in death penalty trials and appeals. She lives in Columbia, where she has planted lots of trees and neighborhood gardens and played piano and organ at her church for nearly forty years.

Orangeburg native KATE SALLEY PALMER started doing political cartoons for the *Greenville News* in 1975. In 1980 the (now renamed) Field Newspaper Syndicate began distributing her cartoons nationwide. Recipient of the 1981 Freedoms Foundations George Washington medal for editorial cartooning, Palmer began writing and illustrating picture books in 1989 and has illustrated more than twenty for major publishers. Warbranch Press, Inc., is the publishing company she and her husband, Jim, formed in 1998. Palmer has produced ten titles for Warbranch Press: a reissue of Simon & Schuster's *A Gracious Plenty; The Pink House; The Little*

Chairs; Palmetto: Symbol of Courage; Francis Marion and the Legend of the Swamp Fox (illustrated by Jim and Kate's son, James); *Almost Invisible: Black Patriots of the American Revolution; First South Carolinians* (also illustrated by James Palmer), *I Know Santa Very Well;, Hostie,* and her latest book, *2016: Race for the White House, a Grownup Coloring Book.* In 2006 the Clemson University Digital Press published her memoir/cartoon retrospective, *Growing Up Cartoonist in the Baby Boom South.*

JOHN W. PILLEY JR. is an Emeritus professor of Psychology at Wofford College in Spartanburg. His groundbreaking research with his dog Chaser, known as "The Smartest Dog in the World," has been featured on *Nova ScienceNOW, 60 Minutes,* NBC's *Today Show, CBS Sunday Morning, CBS World News Tonight with Diane Sawyer,* and *Nat Geo Wild,* among others. Pilley has been working with Chaser since 2004 and has published his scientific findings from this work in the Elsevier journals *Behavioral Processes* and *Learning and Motivation.* He is a *New York Times* bestselling author of *Chaser, Unlocking the Genius of the Dog Who Knows 1000 Words.* His work has been featured in the *New York Times, Wall Street Journal, Paris Match, The Daily Mail, Washington Post, Time Magazine, People Magazine,* and other periodicals in more than 72 countries. For more information, visit www.chasertherbordercollie.com.

JON PINEDA was born in Charleston. He is the author of the novel *Let's No One Get Hurt* (Farrar, Straus and Giroux, 2018) and the poetry collection *Little Anodynes,* winner of the 2016 Library of Virginia Literary Award in Poetry. His other books include the novel *Apology,* winner of the 2013 Milkweed National Fiction Prize, the memoir *Sleep in Me,* a 2010 Barnes & Noble Discover Great New Writers Selection, and the poetry collections *The Translator's Diary,* winner of the 2007 Green Rose Prize in Poetry, and *Birthmark,* winner of the 2003 Crab Orchard Award Series in Poetry Open Competition. He lives in Virginia and teaches at the University of Mary Washington and in the low-residency MFA program at Queens University of Charlotte.

MARK POWELL is the author of five novels, most recently *Small Treasons,* by Gallery/Simon and Schuster. He has received fellowships from the National Endowment for the Arts, the Breadloaf and Sewanee Writers' Conferences, and in 2014 was a Fulbright Fellow to Slovakia. He lives in the mountains of North Carolina and teaches at Appalachian State University.

BERNARD E. POWERS JR. earned a PhD in American history at Northwestern University. He has been employed in higher education more than thirty years and is professor of history at the College of Charleston, where he teaches courses in American, African American, and African diasporic history. His major work, *Black Charlestonians: A Social History 1822–1885,* was designated an Outstanding Academic Book by *Choice* magazine. His most recent article, "'The Worst of All

Barbarism': Racial Anxiety and the Approach of Secession in the Palmetto State," was published in the *South Carolina Historical Magazine*. Powers currently is researching the rise of black Methodism in South Carolina and with Herb Frazier and Marjory Wentworth is author of *We Are Charleston: Tragedy and Triumph at Mother Emanuel*. A Chicago native, he lives in Charleston.

Award-winning writer/photographer PAT ROBERTSON has been published in numerous newspapers, magazines, and websites. He wrote an outdoors column in the *Columbia Record* and the *State* newspapers for more than thirty years. He and his wife, Jan, live in Blythewood, where they raise and train beagles and compete in beagle field trials. He has many fond memories of fishing Stevens Creek with his grandfather, the late C. L. Bridges of Clarks Hill.

SALLIE ANN ROBINSON is a celebrity chef, television personality, and author of *Gullah Home Cooking the Daufuskie Way* and *Cooking the Gullah Way: Morning, Noon, and Night*. As well as working as a private chef and caterer across the United States, Robinson is a certified nursing assistant. Back home on Daufuskie Island after years in Savannah, she is leading Gullah history tours, catering private dinners and parties, and nursing.

AÏDA ROGERS is a writer and editor whose feature journalism has won national and regional awards. After many years of working in print journalism, she now writes and edits for the Honors College at her alma mater, the University of South Carolina. A Lexington native, Rogers lives in Columbia and McClellanville with her husband, his boats, and their dogs.

JONATHAN SANCHEZ grew up in Charlotte and went to West Charlotte High School and then Yale University. The author of the short story collection *Bandit* (2005), Sanchez is a two-time winner in the S.C. Fiction Project and a former writer-in-residence at the Kerouac House in Orlando. He lives in Charleston with his wife and family, where he wrangles the three-headed beast that is Blue Bicycle Books, YALLFest young adult book festival, and Write of Summer, a writing camp for kids.

ALEX SANDERS has been a lawyer, a legislator, a state senator, chief judge of the South Carolina Court of Appeals, and the president of the College of Charleston. He was graduated from the University of South Carolina and the University of Virginia. Sanders is the author of a number of law-related and baseball-related publications, including "Newgarth Revisited: Mrs. Robinson's Case," "The Worst Jury Argument I Ever Made," and "How Baseball United America after the Civil War." He also is the author of one article on both law and baseball, "William S. Stevens (1948–2008) and the Common Law Origins of the Infield Fly Rule." He lives in Charleston with long-suffering Zoe, his wife of more than fifty years.

MARTHA R. SEVERENS served as curator of the Greenville County Museum of Art 1992–2010, having held similar positions at the Gibbes Museum of Art in Charleston and the Portland (Maine) Museum of Art. She holds a master's degree in art history from Johns Hopkins University. Her most recent publications include a monograph, *More Than a Likeness: The Enduring Art of Mary Whyte*, and she is the co-author of *Scenic Impression: Southern Interpretations from the Johnson Collection*, and *Reynolda: Her Muses, Her Stories*.

JIM WELCH began his professional career as a television journalist at the NBC affiliate in Honolulu, Hawaii, and was for eight years the anchor and producer for newscasts on WIS-TV in Columbia. At the SCETV network he wrote, produced, and hosted hundreds of specials, documentaries, and series, including the nationally televised *NatureScene*. Born on a Vermont farm, Welch has spent the lion's share of his life in his adopted state of South Carolina.

After suffering a severe back injury playing football at the University of South Carolina, H. A. (HUMPY) WHEELER turned to writing, covering sports for the *State* and *Columbia Record* newspapers in Columbia. He won his first writing contest in 1960, chronicling Hank Aaron's experiences traveling as a black man in the still-segregated South for the *Columbia Record*. Wheeler is best known for his thirty-five year career as president of the Charlotte Motor Speedway and for his work promoting NASCAR. He has been inducted into fourteen halls of fame, including those for International Motorsports, American Motorsports, Carolinas Boxing, and the colleges of communications at the University of South Carolina and the University of North Carolina. With Peter Golenbock, Wheeler is the author of *Growing Up NASCAR: Racing's Most Outrageous Promoter Tells All* (2009), and *The Mechalete* (1981), which became the first physical fitness manual for race-car drivers in history. He has been honored by four governors of North Carolina for his work advancing tourism and won more than twenty national and international awards for his work in sports promotion, including the 2005 Pius Award, given annually to the one sports person in the world who helped advance Christianity, grace in winning and losing, and respect in professional and amateur sports. He lives in Charlotte, North Carolina, and on Seabrook Island, South Carolina.

Recipient of the Elizabeth O'Neill Verner Award from the South Carolina Arts Commission, watercolor artist MARY WHYTE is a teacher and author whose figurative paintings have earned national recognition, including the Portrait Society of America's Gold Medal in 2016. A resident of Johns Island, Whyte garners much of her inspiration from the Gullah descendants of enslaved coastal Carolinians who number among her most prominent subjects. Her portraits are included in numerous corporate, private, and university collections, as well as in the permanent collections of South Carolina's Greenville County Museum of Art and the

Gibbes Museum of Art in Charleston. Her paintings have been featured in *International Artist, Artist, American Artist, Watercolor, American Art Collector, L'Art de l'Aquarelle,* and numerous other publications. Whyte is the author of *Alfreda's World,* a compilation of her Gullah paintings, as well as *An Artist's Way of Seeing, Watercolor for the Serious Beginner,* and *Down Bohicket Road: An Artist's Journey.* Her work is available through marywhyte.com.

Poet-teacher JANE FLOYD ZENGER, PhD, has worked in the fields of reading, writing, and literacy in China, Zambia, Texas, and South Carolina. Her academic research has been published in numerous scholarly education journals and her early poems in *From the Green Horseshoe: Poems by James Dickey's Students.* A feature writer and poetry editor for *Auntie Bellum,* South Carolina's first feminist magazine, she also edited the *Spotlight,* a journal dedicated to at-risk youth, teen pregnancy and dropout prevention. A Florence native, Zenger has been a featured poet in various venues including Mind Gravy, White Rose Crossing and Magnify Magnolias. She currently is working on a book of poetry based on love, redemption and traveling under the radar in third world countries.